ROUTLEDGE LIBRARY EDITIONS:
PSYCHOLOGY OF EDUCATION

Volume 13

PEER COUNSELLING IN SCHOOLS

PEER COUNSELLING IN SCHOOLS

a time to listen

Edited by
HELEN COWIE AND SONIA SHARP

Routledge
Taylor & Francis Group
LONDON AND NEW YORK

First published in 1996 by David Fulton Publishers Ltd

This edition first published in 2018
by Routledge
2 Park Square, Milton Park, Abingdon, Oxon OX14 4RN

and by Routledge
711 Third Avenue, New York, NY 10017

Routledge is an imprint of the Taylor & Francis Group, an informa business

British Library Cataloguing in Publication Data
A catalogue record for this book is available from the British Library

ISBN: 978-1-138-24157-2 (Set)
ISBN: 978-1-315-10703-5 (Set) (ebk)
ISBN: 978-1-138-28003-8 (Volume 13) (hbk)
ISBN: 978-1-315-27614-4 (Volume 13) (ebk)

Publisher's Note
The publisher has gone to great lengths to ensure the quality of this reprint but points out that some imperfections in the original copies may be apparent.

Disclaimer
The publisher has made every effort to trace copyright holders and would welcome correspondence from those they have been unable to trace.

Peer Counselling in Schools

a time to listen

Edited by
Helen Cowie
and Sonia Sharp

David Fulton Publishers
London

David Fulton Publishers Ltd
2 Barbon Close, London WC1N 3JX

First published in Great Britain by David Fulton Publishers 1996

British Library Cataloguing in Publication Data

A catalogue record for this book is available from the British Library

ISBN 1-85346-367-1

Typeset by Textype Typesetters, Cambridge
Printed in Great Britain by the Cromwell Press Ltd, Melksham

Contents

Acknowledgements

This book arises from the Peer Counselling Research Project based at The Roehampton Institute London, and funded by the Calouste Gulbenkian Foundation. We would like to acknowledge the energy and initiative of the research team, Lucy Brooks, Clare Murray, Ginny Farmiloe and Don Briggs, whose efforts also helped produce the *Peer Counselling Networker*. This newsletter gave us access to practitioners and researchers in the UK, Australia, New Zealand, Canada, USA, Portugal, Spain and Hungary, and enabled us to make contact with the innovators at the heart of this movement. These contacts were invaluable in the preparation of the book. We hope that in a small way we were able to facilitate links among those who wish to know more about the potential of young people to help and support one another through difficulties.

We would like to thank the teachers and peer counsellors who gave their time generously and answered our questions patiently. We hope that in the book you will find useful examples of peer counselling and support systems and a sense of the dedication of the people who work together in this challenging field.

Preface

Why does peer counselling matter? We believe that peer support begins with the natural willingness of most young people to act in a cooperative, friendly way towards one another. Peer counselling and support systems build on this intrinsic quality and create structures which facilitate the young person's potential for responsible, sensitive, empathic caring. We are not denying that conflict exists or that some will misuse the power which they have over vulnerable peers. At the same time, adults need to acknowledge that young people have something distinctive to offer their peers in distress. They are often there at the very time when the difficulty arises. At that point, instead of passively standing by and watching, or actively colluding with those who contribute to the problem, they can reach out to offer understanding, friendship, and time to listen. If the reason for not being supportive at that moment arises from fear of retaliation, lack of confidence, anxiety about being rebuffed or a concern that the right words may be hard to find, then we as adults need to learn how to offer these young people the opportunity to practise the skills of helping and the confidence to believe in the quality of the helping relationship which they would like to give.

How can adults support peer counselling initiatives? In Part I, *Understanding and Preparing for Peer Support*, we give guidelines, all rooted in practice and research, to teachers, social workers, education welfare officers, educational psychologists and other professionals involved in the pastoral care and well-being of young people. We have illustrated the positive outcomes for helpers, for those who are helped and for the school community as a whole. We have provided examples of training workshops which disseminate the skills of the active listener, and the skills of the mediator. We have not neglected the importance of supervision which underpins the development of the reflective practitioner and which provides the safe place where difficulties may be shared and ethical dilemmas confronted. We have presented the framework of the whole-school policy as an enabling structure within which peer counselling can more readily flourish. In Part II, *Peer Counselling and Support in Action*, the practitioners give their own accounts of the peer counselling and support initiatives which they have developed in a range of settings. Some emphasise befriending, some adopt a counselling approach, others mediate between peers whose relationships with one another are disturbed or disturbing. We hear the voices of the teachers as they reflect on the processes of helping and we hear from the peer helpers themselves as they describe the costs and benefits of their work. Finally in Part III, *Peer Counselling and Support: Evaluating its Impact*, we address the issue of evaluation, firstly by recommending a variety of methods for assessing the impact of an intervention on the members of a school community, and secondly by examining the broader issues which face researchers as they investigate the nature of the helping relationship – its outcomes, processes and structures.

Helen Cowie and Sonia Sharp
January 1996

Part I

Understanding and Preparing for Peer Support

CHAPTER 1

Overview

When a child is born he/she is loving, lovable, intelligent, creative, energetic, powerful, gentle, sociable and cooperative. We never lose these qualities; because they are the essence of being human. Our bodies age, but the child within each of us remains the same. Each night the stars are shining, even though on some nights they cannot be seen because of the clouds. So it is with the child within us. What must be done, then, is for the clouds, which have accumulated along the way, to be cast off. And then the stars within us will shine with all their brilliance. (Marthaler in Frey, 1991)

Introduction

Counselling is commonly defined as an activity in which a trained professional engages in a particular relationship with a person who is experiencing personal or emotional difficulties. The idea of empowering young people to offer support to peers in distress can at first glance be viewed with suspicion by professionals in the field. Typical comments at a recent conference included:

"These pupils are too young to understand complex emotions."
"They could do damage."
"What about the confidentiality?"
"It takes years of training and experience to do this work."
"Who would ultimately be responsible if something went wrong?"
"They would never have the patience and stamina to keep it going."

But are these understandable doubts justified? Throughout this book we argue that the largely untapped resource of peer support and help should be taken more seriously. For one thing, there is much evidence to show that the presence of close, intimate relationships with members of our peer group can fend off the worst effects of stress (Duck, 1991); furthermore, when we are in difficulty, it is to peers – people of a similar age group or those who have shared the same experience – that we often turn initially for help, support and understanding. Peers share with us a distinctive history and a particular social context, and peers are often willing to give their time and to offer themselves in the role of listener and supporter at the very point of crisis when the professional help is simply not available. However well-meaning the adults may be, the young person in distress may never actually approach the expert who could offer help. Furthermore, we as adults often underestimate the capacity of young people to empathise with one another's suffering and to offer helpful support and guidance.

So, the term "peer counselling" is used in this book in a broad sense, not to describe a specialist activity involving highly trained professionals but as an extension of the very natural willingness, evident in most social groups, to offer help, support and a listening ear to others in the same or a similar age-group. In the course of the book, you will read about research into peer counselling, you will discover the practicalities of setting it up in school contexts, and you will have the opportunity to overview case studies of peer counselling in action. But before we embark on this, we need to find out something of the nature of peer support systems, what they are, how they have arisen and where they flourish.

Animal studies

We look first at relevant biological studies of conflict, aggression and reconciliation among primates to see if the parallels which can be drawn between the social world of animals and that of humans give insights into why humans are cruel and rejecting in some settings and cooperative and supportive in others.

De Waal (1992) suggests that, in primate society, the complex interplay between aggression and cooperation contributes constructively to social relationships within the group. If we look at animals in their social context, he points out, we certainly see planned violence. For example, the chimps in the Gombe observed by Goodall (1986) stalked their enemies, attacked and eliminated them with extreme brutality. There is no doubt that this kind of violence exists. Yet if we look more closely, we can see that the aggressive behaviour is closely interwoven with acts of conciliation and support. In his detailed observations of chimpanzees in the Yerkes Regional Primate Research Center, De Waal found that, in comparison with other types of interaction, "food encounters" were characterised by increased levels of both aggressive and appeasement behaviour. For example, out of 4,653 interactions concerning food, over half involved a transfer of food *from* one chimpanzee *to* another. The rate of sharing by A with B was balanced by a reciprocal sharing by B with A ($r=0.552$, $p< 0.001$). During these types of encounter, there was a more than 100-fold increase in the rate of calming body contact such as kissing, touching and embracing, and only a ninefold increase in aggression. In other words, there were many more instances of sharing and cooperating than of aggression. And the aggression, when it appeared, was selective. Those chimps who had not shown themselves to be generous in sharing found that, when they came to their fellows for food, they were more likely to be treated to an aggressive rebuff. The chimps demonstrated through the selective nature of their aggressive responses to others that they had some concept of injustice, unfairness and lack of reciprocity and a need to promote egalitarian food sharing relationships.

In a study of aggressive encounters between pigtail macaques, Judge (1991) observed "third party" reconciliations. Here individuals not involved in the conflict demonstrated affiliative acts with the aggressor. These individuals included kin of both aggressor and victim, and the behaviour could be seen as an attempt to conciliate the aggressor or to reconcile the two in conflict. There is also evidence, in studies of chimp interaction after a conflict (Smucny and Aureli, 1994), of contacts between bystanders and the victim which appear to demonstrate attempts on the part of the bystanders to console the injured party.

These observations in the field suggest that primates possess powerful mechanisms of reassurance and reconciliation which allow them to cope with the socially negative effects of aggression within their own social group. "As a result, aggression can be a well-integrated part of, and can contribute constructively to, social relationships" (De Waal, 1992, p. 53).

Can this research cast light on our thinking about peer counselling? It is certainly of interest to us to know that primatologists are currently concerned to find answers to the following questions. Are there post-conflict interactions involving members of the peer group? How do peers respond to aggressors and victims in the aftermath of dispute? Do peers and bystanders have a role to play in reconciling the two parties in a conflict, in consoling the loser and in appeasing the aggressor?

4

Siblings: cooperation and conflict

The growing body of research evidence indicating the importance of sibling relationships across the life span also offers useful insights into our understanding of peer relationships. Most psychologists accept that individuals' experiences with parents in the early years affect the quality of their relationships with others. There are different explanations for this: psychodynamic theory (e.g. Winnicott, 1984), attachment theory (Bowlby, 1988; Main *et al.*, 1985) and family systems (Minuchin, 1974), for example. But fewer theories acknowledge the full impact of the quality of the relationship with siblings on a person's capacity to relate with others. Most of us grow up in families where there is at least one sibling and, in fact, by the time they are a year old, most children will spend as much time with their siblings as they do with their mothers (Dunn, 1983). The relationship is a unique one and it has a special status within the family. Siblings get to know one another intimately and, as Dunn's work has shown, children demonstrate sensitivity and empathy for their siblings far in advance of expectations based on traditional theories of child development. Older siblings have been shown to adopt roles as varied as attachment figure (Stewart, 1983), caregiver (Weissner and Gallimore, 1977), tutor (Cicirelli, 1976) and playmate (Katz *et al.*, 1992). There is conflict in the relationships among siblings but, as Katz *et al.* (1992) have shown in their review, these conflicts may facilitate social development because children have a fairly safe context in which to practise ways of responding to conflict, aggression and distressing feelings. Children also report that their siblings are a source of alliance, companionship and intimacy. In fact, Barnes and Austin (1991) showed in their research that children's perceptions of sibling warmth were good predictors of their self-esteem – more so than maternal warmth and sensitivity.

Dunn found that negative life events such as difficulty at school or an illness in the family brought siblings closer together and that they were likely to provide one another with emotional support during these times of crisis. In fact, many people seem to report that they grow closer to their siblings as they progress through life and many report that a sibling is a close friend (Ross and Milgram, 1982).

Dunn's pioneering research on siblings (1983; 1988) has demonstrated that the interactions between young children and a sibling are qualitatively different from those between child and parent. She noted in her naturalistic observations of children in their home settings that younger siblings, early in the second year of life, showed a clear grasp of how to annoy or comfort the other child. Her work led to a model of the growth of social understanding in which the child's development as a social being grows out of his or her responsiveness to the feelings and behaviour of others. Dunn argues that significant contributions to the child's development in the family context are made by intense self-concern on the one hand and with "participation in the moral discourse of the family" on the other.

Of particular relevance to our work on peer counselling is Dunn's finding in her follow-up study of the siblings whom she had observed as pre-schoolers (Dunn *et al.*, 1991). When she and her colleagues revisited these children in middle childhood and adolescence, they found that there were links between the quality of the relationships between the siblings in the pre-school period and the children's behaviour at a later age. For example, those who had grown up with a sibling who had been unfriendly or aggressive were more likely as adolescents to have emotional difficulties in their relationships with others than those whose siblings had been warm and affectionate to them.

There are also interesting inter-generational effects. Researchers looking at the basis for children's friendships have looked to the wider context of the family. Putallaz *et al.* (1991) found that children are influenced by their mother's recollection of her own childhood (including her own recall of sibling relationships). It seems that this recollection affects the ways in which she prepares her children for the peer relationships which they will have at school. Kramer and Baron (1995) investigated whether there is a close relationship between parents' reports of their childhood sibling relationships, their current parenting goals and behaviours, and the quality of their own children's relationships; they found that there was not a simple linear relationship between individuals' childhood sibling relationships and experiences and the quality of their children's sibling relationships. In other words, there was the possiblity of discontinuity between parenting beliefs and behaviours across generations. Their research suggests that we need to know more about the coping strategies and the qualities of resilience which some individuals acquire in order to avoid the problems which they become enmeshed in as children.

However, this research would suggest that experience with siblings has a strong impact on individuals' capacity to understand relationships and on the ways in which they interact socially with their peers.

6

Why do peers help one another?

Conflict and cooperation are woven into the complex web of relationships which children and adolescents form with their peers, and learning how to understand the many facets of their social world is an essential part of growing up. The following accounts by children (taken from Cowie *et al.*, 1994) indicate that children vary widely in their capacity to become skilled navigators in the sea of interpersonal relationships. Here Ben, aged 10, describes how he deals with quarrels with his best friend:

> We do quarrel but we usually make it up. Sometimes we have an argument and then next time we meet we forget about it. It's in the past and it doesn't matter any more. I don't have too many friends. If I had millions of friends and I had an argument with him I could walk off. But instead I try to make it up with him. (Cowie *et al.*, 1994, p. 1)

Children can demonstrate sensitivity and empathy for a friend but can also tolerate a certain level of conflict within the relationship. Laursen (1993), in a study of adolescent conflicts, found that disagreements with friends and partners were associated with lower levels of negative affect, higher levels of continued social interaction and improved relations after the dispute. Laursen suggests that most adolescents learn to manage conflicts in such a way as to minimise their disruptive effects. In the context of an existing friendship, conflict can play an important part in maintaining the relationship and even in strengthening it. Positive outcomes can include ego development, enhanced understanding of relationships and the realignment of roles.

But the peer group can also behave in ways which are deliberately designed to cause pain and hurt, and conflicts can have damaging effects on the group as well as on the individual (Hartup, 1992; Selman, 1980). Alan, a bully-victim aged 9, is frequently involved in fights and quarrels, some of which he initiates himself. He does not like members of his class on the whole and assumes, quite accurately, that many of them do not like him in return. But some peers are able to show awareness of his situation. Here Shoukat, who has already experienced victimisation in the class, describes his upset when he sees Alan being bullied:

> Alan, he's like Saleem, like when Saleem's at school, I think he's a bit scared from inside ... Yeah, he's scared inside, because the other day we were lining up and everyone just started pushing him I don't know why. And then they pushed him off the chair and he fell on the floor – teacher weren't there – and they all started kicking him and kicking him. Children from our class – I

> don't know why – they get bad-tempered. They are a real laugh but they get bad-tempered. And they were doing this to him. When Miss said, "Who were the first to hit Alan?" I looked at some of these people ... If they really wanted to beat Alan up they wouldn't volunteer [i.e. admit to having done it], but they did. They volunteered and they said, "We're really sorry. We won't do it again." (Cowie *et al.*, 1994, pp. 176–7)

Shoukat had not felt able to protest at the time but he did go up to Alan afterwards and offer him genuine support based on his empathy for the suffering which Alan was experiencing. This support continued when similar incidents took place and, although Alan remained a target of bullying in the class at large, at least in small group settings with peers like Shoukat he was offered a haven. In the longer term this enabled Alan to experience some positive relationships with peers which improved the quality of his social life.

Even for those who, like Shoukat, do not want to cause their peers to feel rejected and unwanted, there may be strong pressure from the peer group not to intervene. The awareness of another's suffering may then never be expressed and the victim may not realise that others care about him or her. The impact on self-esteem can be catastrophic. The peer group is important to the young person and lack of acknowledgement or affirmation from that social group can lead to the internalisation of profound feelings of unworthiness, loneliness and despair. Often children want to help others who are in distress but don't know how.

Some researchers have looked at the phenomenon of peer helping in terms of costs and benefits and try to explain how it comes about that apparently self-sacrificing behaviour – where the helper incurs a "cost" – persists and is not eliminated through natural selection. McGuire (1994) points out that since helping often occurs between people who already know one another (that is, who are not strangers to one another), the helping is likely to be influenced by longer-term social considerations such as reciprocity and enhanced reputation in the social group. It seems that there *can* be benefits to those who offer help. Social mediators, such as increased self-esteem, the development of empathy, the internalisation of social norms and values, can evoke and encourage helping behaviour. In school settings, the broader social benefits of peer counselling might arise from an enhanced social climate in the school community as a whole; the immediate benefits to the individual helper would derive from being an active member of a group which shared a commitment to qualities such as kindness, sharing and being helpful.

Other researchers consider the intrinsic worth of helping behaviours from the earliest months of life. They argue that humans have a strong inborn motivation to form cooperative, supportive relationships with one another. Even very young children actively seek out cooperation with others. The strategy of reaching out to special others in a spirit of trust is universal, though the ways in which it is expressed will vary from culture to culture. Children learn about how to act towards others by engaging in shared activities and the meanings which they develop arise out of their search for sense and order in a community of people working and living together. Up to a point it is helpful for the developing child to experience conflict and to become aware of strategies for dealing with it. However, if children are reared in an environment where there is excessive violence, lack of affection, little valuing of the person, they will develop "a defensive adaptation that cripples their curiosity and imagination. They become unsociable, uncultured, specialised in survival and remorseless in exploitation of others" (Trevarthen and Logotheti, 1989, p. 177).

Peer relationships

Peer relationships are extremely important for the young people concerned and the effects of the quality of relationships with the peer group can endure right into adulthood. If they were good and if the young person succeeded in coping with conflicts which arose, it is likely that they will be well-prepared for relationships in adulthood. However, if the experience was a bad one, there may well be long-term problems. Conceptions of friendship change over time from a concern with shared activities through to mutual trust and cooperation during childhood to an emphasis on intimacy and mutual understanding during adolescence.

During the middle years of childhood, most children learn to negotiate with one another over areas of conflict. As we have seen, children and adolescents, even when they are good friends, can conflict with one another. But this conflict is not inevitably linked with aggression and disruption. Rather, it seems to be the case that conflicts are typically resolved by the young people themselves and that through this process they learn important things about themselves, their peers and about relationships with others. The resolution of arguments, disagreements, oppositions and refusals to cooperate can offer young people the opportunity to engage in social problem solving since they need to interpret social behaviour, identify their own social goals and find socially acceptable ways of attaining them. Shantz (1983) considers that social problem solving is one of the most important dimensions of social competence. The ability of children and adolescents to take the perspective of others changes over time and offers an essential basis for effective functioning in the social world. Children who are antisocial (for example, those who abuse their power) tend to be delayed in their capacity to take the perspective of others.

Cowie *et al.*, (1994) consider two primary dimensions of social relationships – affiliation and power. Children who are neglected by their peers, especially if this situation continues throughout school, may be timid or socially unskilled. This causes great unhappiness and loneliness and can have severe long-term effects on their capacity to form close friendships with others. Duck (1991) notes that if you are unpopular at school, you are more likely to become as an adult someone who has interpersonal difficulties. Children who are rejected – that is, who are actively disliked by peers – are even more at risk. Some are rejected because they are aggressive and disruptive (like Alan in the case study quoted on pages 6–7). Self-esteem affects the ways in which children interact with others – in the longer term this can affect their social success or lack of success in adult life.

The second primary dimension of social relationships is power. There will always be power relationships in social groups since one person may be physically stronger or intellectually more knowledgeable than another. That person is then more likely to take the lead within the group. Problems arise, however, when that power is abused, as, for example, when the stronger person takes advantage of his or her power to cause harm or distress to another. The systematic abuse of power is central to bullying behaviour, a major cause of distress amongst young people in school settings which causes psychological damage to both the individual and the school community at large (Besag, 1989; Olweus, 1994; Smith and Sharp, 1994).

Cooperation amongst members of the peer group is not synonymous with friendship but it does mean the existence of relationships based on fairness, reciprocity and tolerance. While it is possible to cooperate with someone without actually being their friend, it is also true that cooperation is one important precondition of friendship. However, while cooperation can lead to friendship, it need not do so. In this sense, cooperation is "an active state of mind which does not avoid conflict" (Cowie *et al.*, 1994, p. 192).

Learning about social responsibility

There is a moral dimension to this discussion. In becoming self-aware, children and young people are engaging in a process of learning about significant relationships and social roles. By cooperating with others in a social group which is important to them, young people gain direct experience of learning about what is morally right for that group as well as the opportunity to learn when reciprocity is of greater value than the maximisation of individual benefits. Schools are in a position to create opportunities for pupils to experience what Carr (1991) calls "positive participative citizenship" (p. 374) and peer counselling appears to be one way in which this aim might be achieved. Carr observes that the ideal of positive participatory citizenship is in harmony with a moral model of democracy incorporating the following range of democratic practices (adapted from p. 379).

Core principle

Democracy is intrinsically justified. It is a way of life in which people are able to realise their human potential by participating actively in the life of their society. Citizens in such a society enjoy equal opportunities for self-development, self-fulfilment and self-determination.

Key features

It is a moral ideal and so is never truly achieved. It requires continuously expanding opportunities for participation of all citizens in decision-making by bringing social, political, industrial and economic institutions under genuine democratic control.

Main assumptions

Human beings are essentially political and social. They are fulfilled by taking part in the common life of their community. All should have the right to participate in debates about the good of the society. The distinction between rulers and ruled is one of degree rather than kind.

Social conditions

Democracy can only flourish in a society in which there is a knowledgeable and informed citizenry which is capable of engaging in public decision-making and political debate on equal terms. In such a society, bureaucratic control over public life is minimal and decision-making is not treated as a form of professional expertise.

This model is moral in the sense that it is founded on intrinsic human values of self-fulfilment, self-determination and equality; furthermore, it prescribes the moral principles of a society which claims to be democratic. To Carr, "the task of cultivating in pupils the knowledges, skills and attitudes necessary for this kind of public participation is the only way of providing an education which enables them to fulfil their status as citizens" (p. 381). Schools can facilitate this process by creating structures which actively promote participative involvement on the part of young people. The adoption of such approaches will play a part in enabling the development of responsibility in young people and the capacity to take the perspective of others. This is important if pupils are to develop into adults with an active approach towards their own community. At the heart of this is the valuing of democratic procedures and the sharing of responsibility.

In all cultures the motives for mutual benefit are very powerful. It is only when cooperative motives are frustrated or cheated that selfish motives gain the upper hand. Cultures vary greatly in the extent to which they train young people to develop qualities of helping and support for one another, and we still need to learn more about how children become socialised into cooperative social life and about the range of ways in which families and societies differ in their patterns of dealing with anger, hurt, fear, suspicion, hostility. In our culture, peer counselling offers young people an opportunity to practise and develop these capacities and to gain experience of different roles and responsibilities. In the next chapter, we explore some of the forms which peer support can take.

CHAPTER 2

What is Peer Counselling?

There have recently been concerted attempts to harness the capacity which peers have to console, appease, befriend one another, to mediate in conflicts and to reconcile those who are alienated from one another. As we have seen, in adolescence, young people in distress often turn first to a peer for help. A growing body of evidence suggests that, with the right sort of training and support, it is possible to create systems which facilitate this natural process and which build on the potential for helping which is already there. In a very broad sense we can call this *peer counselling*. Peer counselling seems to flourish in settings where there is an already established system for working together and in cooperation with one another (Carr, 1994) and where people support the values of caring about others and helping people to help themselves. It helps too if there is a concern for and a belief in relationships that are based on equality and mutuality coupled with a dislike of relationships based on hierarchies. For a peer counselling programme to be sustained over time, it is also important that pioneering individuals in the organisation are committed to its development. One characteristic of these individuals is an interest in innovation or changes in human systems. In Carr's words:

> They assess needs; they listen; they involve; they support; they model; they encourage; and they rebuild. They actually study how innovations take place and they implement the strategies and actions that contribute to making changes. (Carr, 1994, p. 7)

But what do we mean by peer counselling? Carr (1994) has counted over 30 different terms to define peer helping programmes, ranging from peer ambassadors to peer facilitators to peer helpers. In his survey of members of the Canadian National Peer Network, Carr found that 38 per cent use the term peer helper; 35 per cent use the term peer counsellor; 12 per cent use the term peer support worker; 2 per cent use the term peer facilitators and the remaining 13 per cent use terms including peer tutor, peer assistant and peer educator.

In the next section we argue that there are three broad types of peer counselling and support, each overlapping to an extent with one another – befriending, counselling approaches and conflict resolution. Unlike Carr, we have not included peer tutoring since this is more closely linked to cognitive processes of learning.

Befriending

The practice of befriending, although it can take a variety of forms, is usually focussed on enabling the pupils to apply the skills of helping in everyday interactions with peers. They may play an active part in befriending pupils who are new to the school and be involved in the induction programmes set up by the school. In other forms of befriending, peers can play an active part in after-school clubs or in serving breakfasts for pupils who arrive early at school and who would otherwise be at a loose end (Konet, 1991). An important role can also be to assist at parents' evenings in order to promote and publicise the service which they offer. They may be assigned as "buddies" to peers who have been referred by teachers concerned that they are, for example, lonely or neglected by classmates (Henrikson, 1991; James *et al.*, 1991). In some programmes, the peer helpers are assigned to a class at set times in order to act as a support to the teacher (Henrikson, 1991). In others, they will help children with learning difficulties or those who seem to have low self-esteem (James *et al.*, 1991). In the Circle of Friends approach (Newton *et al.*, 1996), described in Chapter 6, peers help to create a social network for fellow pupils with emotional and behavioural difficulties. In some cases, groups of young people who have experienced the same or similar difficulties are given the opportunity in a peer group to share feelings such as anger or guilt, and explore areas of particular sensitivity, such as being lonely or rejected by peers. Whatever the form befriending schemes take, the brief for the young people involved is to offer emotional support and friendship to their peers.

Befriending programmes typically aim to:

1 promote personal development in the helpers
2 use peer helpers in the role of caring support for peers
3 have a positive influence on the emotional climate of the school

4 provide a bridge between troubled friends in their peer group and professional counselling services.

Helpers are usually selected on the basis of their personal characteristics and willingness to help others. Depending on the nature of the programme, they may be same-age peers or slightly older. Training is usually focussed on team building among participants and on giving the young people additional knowledge and understanding of the nature of a helping relationship. Typically, training programmes will begin with a period of orientation, sometimes in the form of a one-day or residential workshop, in which the pupils begin the process and learn about the rationale, values and purposes of a helping approach. Follow-up training is usually carried out during class time (for example, during form period), and there will be opportunities for the peer helpers to have debriefing sessions in which they discuss progress, address problems and provide support for one another.

Key research studies of befriending

Research studies of befriending indicate a number of important advantages – for those who are helped, for those who help and for the school environment as a whole. Konet (1991) observed that, through the process of being befriended, young people were given a forum for expressing their feelings about aspects of their lives which were upsetting. They were "given a voice" and this was an important stage in the process of feeling more positive about themselves. Konet observed that:

- helpers begin to learn about how to identify emotional and social problems among their peers and how to begin to resolve them;
- there is a growing awareness of typical issues of concern to peers;
- the helpers gain in qualities of leadership;
- their self-esteem is enhanced.

Henrikson (1991) found significant pre- and post-test differences between the peer helping group and a comparison group. For example, scores on the "Questionnaire for Helpful Responses" increased for the peer helpers ($t=7.25$, $p<0.001$). In addition, there was a significant difference in the expected direction between the befrienders and the comparison group ($f=2.95$, $p<.02$). All of the students but two were successful in learning the helping skill of "empathic responding" as measured by this questionnaire. On qualitative measures, the peer helpers indicated that they had gained in self-knowledge and in confidence as a result of taking part in the programme, and made statements like "I loved it!", "It's sad to leave it" and "It's totally changed the way I respond to my friends; I use the skills *all* the time!"

The school environment has also been shown to change as a result of this kind of peer helping. Henrikson found that the general level of awareness rose amongst students in the school where she did her study, in that over 56 per cent knew how to contact a peer helper if they were in difficulty and almost 50 per cent said that they would consult a peer helper themselves. Amongst teachers, 59 per cent stated that, in their view, the peer helpers were having a positive influence on the climate of the school; 75 per cent rated the peer helpers who had actually worked in their classes in a positive way on criteria such as cooperation, being reliable, setting a good example and relating well to others. Comments included statements like "They have been courteous, helpful, good examples."

Befriending peers with spelling and reading difficulties

James and her colleagues (1991) used a befriending approach to help pupils who were having difficulties with spelling and reading. They chose this particular pupil problem because it is often associated with emotional difficulties. They predicted that, since adolescents are likely to take more notice of the opinions of their peers than of adults, befriending of these pupils by same or similar age peers could have a beneficial effect on both attainment and self-esteem. The researchers were aware, from the research literature and from their own professional experience, that pupils with low attainment in academic subjects often internalise a strong sense of failure. Remedial programmes which are more concerned with the assessment of cognitive deficits may well neglect a consideration of the pupils' self-esteem and feelings of anxiety. In fact, many researchers in this field argue that it is important for children to have a positive self-image as a good speller, and reiterate a common finding that children with learning difficulties often have underlying emotional conflicts or unmet needs which can lead to a cycle of failure and emotional reaction to that failure. One strand of the literature on this field indicates the value of a peer befriending approach in these cases (Murfitt and Thomas, 1983). They considered that such an approach required not necessarily lengthy training but rather the possession of a warm and sympathetic personality. From this perspective, their study investigated the role of sympathetic peers as "therapeutic change agents".

Influenced by this work, James and her colleagues (1991) administered a programme of training to twelve Year 8 secondary pupils (aged 12–13) with spelling difficulties by twelve peer helpers from Years 11 and 12. The twelve pupils to be helped (Group A) were selected from two classes for those with special needs. Twelve other children from the same classes (Group B) were cross-matched on spelling and reading attainment and acted as a control group. The befriending was not planned as a substitute for normal spelling or reading tuition since children in Groups A and B already received this. Befrienders were selected on the basis that they possessed certain qualities, and that they were:

- genuine persons
- real in their own right
- knowing their own feelings
- capable of communicating feelings to others
- able to care for and accept the other person in a non-judgemental way
- possessing an empathic understanding of the other's point of view.

Of the befrienders, eight were able students doing A-level courses; four were pupils who had required special educational support throughout their schooling. The peer helpers were given three one-hour training sessions in which they were introduced to basic techniques – listening attentively, using appropriate facial and body language, asking pertinent questions, making sympathetic comments, being tolerant of silence. Their task was to befriend a pupil for one hour a week, to help these pupils to help themselves and not to tell them what to do.

Initially, they chose an activity of mutual interest like art, pottery or a project. It was stressed that the important thing was the quality of the relationship and not the activity. If the pupil spontaneously expressed feelings of helplessness (for example, "I am hopeless at spelling") the helpers were encouraged to talk about something which *they* had found difficult to master and to explain that by very hard effort they had come to succeed. The pupils were encouraged to accept responsibility for their own future progress, for example by saying "I know, it must have been very difficult for you, it means you have to work twice as hard now to try to catch up." There was no element of tutoring in these encounters.

Excellent relationships were formed and before long the pupils were referring to "my friend". The intervention took place for one hour each week for 20 weeks. Before intervention began, and at the end, standard tests of spelling and reading were administered to the counselled and the control group. The two groups also completed questionnaires on self-concept (Lawrence, 1981) and locus of control (Nowicki and Strickland, 1973).

Evaluation of the intervention showed that, while pupils in the control group maintained their previous rate of progress, the counselled group made significant gains in spelling ($p<0.001$) and in reading ($p<0.05$) These changes are shown in Figures 2.1 and 2.2.

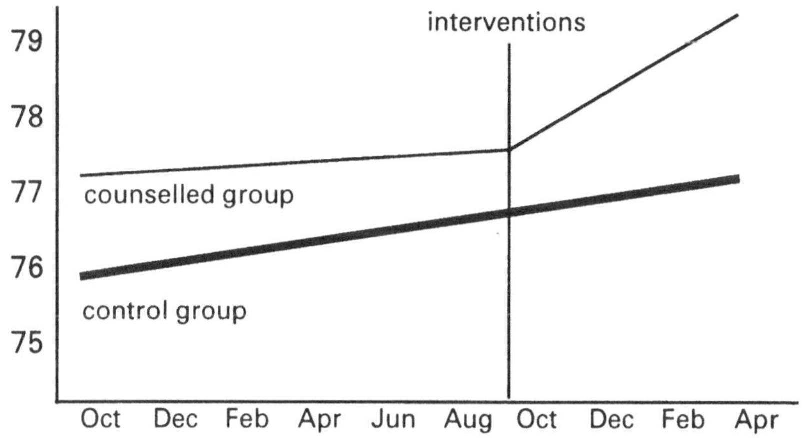

Figure 2.1 Mean reading quotients (out of 100) for Group A, the counselled group, and Group B, the control group

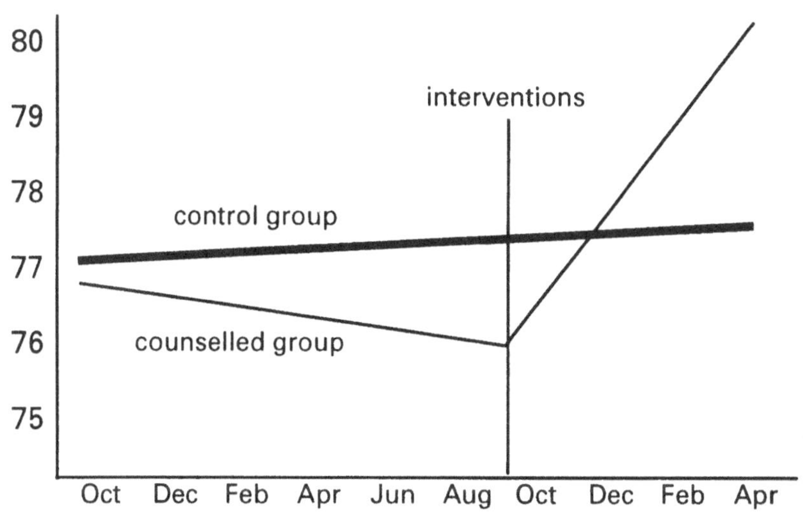

Figure 2.2 Mean spelling quotients for Group A, the counselled group, and Group B, the control group

The differences between the two groups on questionnaire measures of self-concept or locus of control were not statistically significant. However, observations by teachers highlighted an improvement in the counselled group in terms of motivation, effort, handwriting, oral work, self-confidence, attitudes to study and social interaction. Furthermore, the counsellors liked the experience and benefitted from it. They related with increased confidence to teachers when they discussed their part in the project. They showed self-awareness and were able to share insights like a recognition of the value of other pupils, despite their poor academic attainment. They expressed surprise that these pupils, whom they had "looked down on" before, were good at other activities, for example chess or art. They felt that they had gained in their capacity to form constructive relationships with a wider circle of peers. The greatest gain seemed to come in the increased self-esteem of those befrienders who had themselves throughout their school lives needed a lot of guidance and support.

Peer support in bereavement

We turn now to studies which demonstrate the important part to be played by a peer support group in helping young people come to terms with a serious loss through death. Research has shown that the effects of childhood bereavement can last right into adulthood (Marcoux and Kiely, 1985) but there is also evidence that social support from peers can, over time, alleviate the child's distress. For example, Gray (1988) found that 40 per cent of bereaved adolescents reported that the most helpful person at the time of a death was a peer. After the experience of peer counselling, 76 per cent of his participants reported the feeling that peers understood them. Gray also stressed the need for appropriate training, leadership support and supervision during the course of peer support, but his study provides at least anecdotal evidence that the use of a peer support group can greatly alleviate the distress of bereaved adolescents and can help them positively in the mourning process.

Quarmby (1993) gives a useful account of an intervention designed to help bereaved adolescents cope with their loss. Six pupils, three boys and three girls, were asked by senior teachers if they wished to take part. All had experienced the loss of a parent, the deaths occurring between eight and 34 months previously. The group sessions simply involved talking about aspects of the bereavement. Quarmby used pre- and post-counselling interviews with and accounts by participants in the peer counselling sessions, objective measures of anxiety and a behavioural checklist of self-appraisal. His participants reported that the experience during the six sessions had been immensely helpful to them. Through the build-up of mutual trust and the disclosure of painful memories and feelings, participants were able to talk about aspects of their experience which had not previously been shared with anyone. Quarmby notes that the skill of active listening "seemed to come naturally to these young people" (p. 203) and that the atmosphere was one of empathy. The factor which united the group was that all were bereaved so there was a sense in which the other group members understood the difficulties which peers were going through. As one put it:

> Before, when I've talked about my Mum, my friends at home have been really sympathetic, *and it's made it worse!* whereas with X (group member), when I spoke about it, she'd not say – "Are you OK?" – *she knew!* They weren't any better off than me, whereas when I'm talking to my friends at home, I sometimes think – What do they know? They've still got theirs. (Quarmby, 1993, p. 205)

Several trends were noticed in this study. Guilt and anger were more resistant to improvement than other factors. Anxiety for personal health and for the surviving parent were above average. There was also a sense that the bereavement was experienced as leading to a loss of status amongst peers (other than those in the group). Quarmby recommended that schools should make more use of the resource of peers when helping young people through the trauma of the loss of a loved one.

Counselling approaches

We have seen how the natural supportive responses of young people can be harnessed to help peers in distress. In this section, we take it one step further and look at those approaches which adopt a counselling approach in the training and supervision of peer helpers. Here we find a more structured form of helping, including group counselling, telephone counselling and one-to-one counselling. The helpers are trained in well-established counselling skills, including active listening, reflecting back feelings, paraphrasing what the client has said, expressing empathy for the client's emotional state, and developing a vocabulary of feelings (Sharp *et al.*, 1994). These counselling approaches usually include some form of counselling supervision. According to De Rosenroll (1989) such peer support programmes aim to:

1 expand or augment current counselling and support services

2 give young people the enhanced skills to handle peers' developmental and personal issues
3 address the psycho-social needs of a peer group
4 create a more positive community environment.

Peer counsellors have been trained to offer help with such issues as getting on with teachers, relating to the peer group, addressing school bullying, building self-esteem, coping with the transition to a new school, improving body image, and dealing with loneliness.

Training, it is usually acknowledged, must take account of the specific needs of a given population. So typically peer counselling training guides (such as Carr and Saunders, 1980; Tindall and Gray, 1985) incorporate ideas and exercises from a range of sources and will often recommend that practitioners adapt the ideas to suit their own particular context. Training can include such diverse activities as role play, video work, lectures, group work, discussions and pen-and-paper exercises. Peer counsellors usually receive a solid training in fundamental listening and helping skills. Carr and Saunders recommend that this should be 30 hours minimum, but the length of training varies greatly from programme to programme. Peer counsellors may be trained in weekly one-hour sessions, or daily during lunch-hours in a block of ten days, or in weekend retreats. The extent and quality of training tends to depend on the experience and expertise of the trainers, the resources available and the cooperation of the schools concerned. Key issues include the content of the training, the processes which trainees experience, and the qualifications of the trainers.

Only once the peer counsellors are confident in the use of these basic skills should they be offered further training in special issues. Usually, the special issues training will arise from requests on the part of the counsellors themselves. Gougeon (1989) describes how one group of peer counsellors in Canada came to express their need for further training in how to deal with grief and loss. Students identified their own experiences of loss through, for example, parental divorce, break-up of a relationship, move to a new school, death of a friend or family member. They were given the opportunity to be in touch with their feelings surrounding that loss and to gain insights into their own grieving processes, their emotions at the time and the impact of others' responses to them at the time. The trainees brainstormed a long list of loss experiences and then discussed how the grieving process was involved in their own personal reactions to these experiences.

In all cases, it is recommended that the training be experiential, whatever the actual activities are. Presentation of theories of counselling should be kept to a minimum. The most effective training seems to be the kind that gives the trainees the opportunity to share their own experiences and to relate these to the ideas under discussion. In this way, the peer counsellors create their own understanding of the counselling models which they are discovering. All training programmes which use a counselling approach stress the need for the trainers to be attuned to the feelings of participants and to create awareness and understanding of the limits of the trainees' expertise.

Key research studies of counselling approaches

Group counselling

Sprinthall *et al.* (1992) selected 52 students on the basis of their maturity and social skills. They were assigned randomly to an experimental group of 24 students who trained as peer counsellors and a control group of 28 students who were trained as physical education aides. The peer counsellors were given counselling skills training for one semester to run small experiential groups; the training was based on basic counselling skills (Tindall and Gray, 1985) as well as some focussed training. They were also given regular supervision for their work with groups. Of the 24 peer counsellors, ten counselled groups of students from divorced families (E1) and fourteen counselled students from other school settings (E2). The control group were trained to be PE aides and to help younger pupils in a coaching role, but they were not given in-depth counselling skills training, nor did they have the opportunity for guided reflection (supervision). By the end of the programme the researchers found that the two experimental groups differed significantly from the control group on a test of psychological maturity (the Loevinger Sentence Completion Test). The students in the two experimental groups had gained almost a full stage on the Loevinger while the control group remained stable. Qualitative results also illustrated important themes. The peer counsellors at the begining of training focussed on themselves and their own personal issues. By the second semester they were showing a broader perspective and a greater capacity to think and feel about what their clients were experiencing.

The authors point to the following positive effects of peer counselling for both helpers and helped:

1 The clients, middle school students, felt safe to disclose their concerns within the experiential group. One of the benefits of the small group method, they reported, was that they had a chance to find out that other peers were experiencing similar difficulties, with the divorce of their parents, for example. The programme gave them the chance to reflect on these concerns and to see themselves and their families from a new perspective.
2 The helpers too became more mature, showed greater self-awareness and developed in perspective-taking skills. The experience of helping a peer in distress seemed to promote development in thinking and in the capacity to take the perspective of another.
3 Furthermore, it was the opportunity to reflect on the experience in supervision groups which made the difference between the experimental groups and the control group. The control group played a useful role in the school community but lacked the opportunity to reflect on that experience through supervision (in the sense in which it is used in counselling circles).

The adults in this school were impressed by the resourcefulness, insight and responsibility exhibited by the high school helpers. The researchers had worried that the peer counsellors would not be skilled enough to understand the personal complexities of the situations they encountered (Group E1, for example, dealt with the sensitive issue of parental divorce) and not be able to offer the support which their clients needed. They also worried about what the parents would think (even though they had given permission for their children to take part in the study). But in fact, the training and the on-going supervision meetings provided the peer counsellors with the support and skills necessary to run their groups.

Telephone counselling

Boehm and her colleagues (Boehm *et al.*, 1991) document the first year of operation of a peer telephone listening service for adolescents. The Teen Line was established by a church youth group in Toledo, Ohio, modelled on an existing adult crisis line. Twenty-two young people completed a rigorous training programme – an eighteen-hour residential course focussed on community building, issue identification and self-esteem, followed by ten Saturday sessions covering peer relationships, family dynamics, sexuality, suicide, drug and alcohol abuse, and death.

The facilitators were psychiatrists, psychologists, counsellors and ministers. The methods included group discussions, lectures and role play.

The telephones were answered by either two or three teenage phone call answerers (PCAs) with the backup of one adult nightly from 6.00 p.m. to 10.00 p.m. Calls averaged 189 per month, 44 per week and amounted to 2,270 calls over the first year of operation. It was noted that, although 4 per cent of calls dealt with crisis situations such as suicide and physical abuse, 96 per cent were concerned with common adolescent issues such as peer relationships, family dynamics and loneliness.

The researchers concluded that Teen Line is a useful service for junior and senior high school students as shown by the consistent use of the service throughout the year. They noted with some surprise that pregnancy and substance abuse were relatively infrequently the reasons for a call; significant concern was with peer and family relationships and a need to have someone to talk to. These three issues accounted for 62 per cent of calls. This study confirmed earlier work in New Zealand (Hattie, 1975). In Australia, Pearson (1995) also found that the problem areas most frequently reported in a young people's telephone help line were relationship difficulties with peers.

Conflict resolution and mediation

One of the problems with conflict is that, too often, the outcome is that one wins and the other loses. The common interpersonal and intergroup problems – bullying, racist name-calling, fighting – may well escalate if unresolved. The difficulty with punishing wrongdoers is that they are left with feelings of resentment; the behaviour may become even more entrenched; the people who tried to resolve the problem by informing teachers may be labelled as "grassers" and may be worse off than before. In addition, they may never develop sensitivity to the feelings of others or awareness of any sense of responsibility for their actions. A method for the resolution of conflict through peer mediation has evolved from the realisation of the need to create a "win-win" situation.

How does it work? Typically, two trained peer mediators work as a team to encourage problem solving between people who are in disagreement. The mediation process can be carried out where the dispute occurs – often in the playground. Students receive a highly structured programme of training which equips peer helpers with specific skills for mediating in disputes. Training is given in interpersonal skills including active listening, reflection of feelings, clarification, body language, giving "I" messages, types of questioning and effective problem solving. Role playing is used a great deal to practice newly-learned skills such as mediating to resolve quarrels in the playground, or resolving conflict between a child who bullies and one who is bullied.

The rationale is based on the view that conflict is a natural part of human interaction and that training in conflict resolution provides the person with strategies for resolving conflict and, in the longer term, with a deeper understanding of relationships and social interaction. By teaching young people the skills of conflict resolution it is argued that we facilitate the process of personal growth and understanding. The aims of conflict resolution programmes include:

1 developing awareness of the positive nature of conflict
2 learning strategies for resolving conflict
3 applying these strategies to a specific situation
4 developing longer-term approaches to conflict resolution.

Typically, the mediators meet with the disputants, each disputant tells his or her story and how he or she feels about it, the mediators listen carefully without passing judgement, disputants are each asked what they would like to happen, and finally all are involved in exploring what might actually be done. Since the goal of mediation is for disputants to reach an agreement, the question of right and wrong or of assigning blame is less important than a concern with the future behaviour of both of the disputants. Mediation aims to create a win-win situation in which both sides can feel positive about the outcome.

Key studies in conflict resolution and mediation

Several studies have evaluated mediation programmes. Lane *et al.* (1992) reported a marked improvement in behaviour and in the school climate, including a dramatic decrease in self-reported aggressive conflicts, after the introduction of the programme. A significant aspect of the programme was that the regular supervision meetings gave the mediators the opportunity to discuss successes and share problems. This, as well as the success of the interventions, gave the peer mediators practice in sharing and reflecting on experience. For example, one student, an aggressive boy, previously lacking in empathy for his victims, demonstrated his new-found capacity to reflect on experiences in his comment:

> I used to be a bully. I think because I wanted to get the authority – the power. Now, as a conflict manager, I get the authority and status I used to take. I've changed. Now I can feel what the kids feel and I can help them solve their problems. (Lane *et al.*, 1992, p. 19)

Araki *et al.* (1989) found in a Hawaiian high school that, as a result of mediation, the number of on-campus fights dropped from 83 to nineteen over a two-year period. In addition, "at-risk" students who took part in the training and became mediators developed more pro-social attitudes towards conflict. All participants, whether disputants or mediators, became better listeners by taking part in the mediation process since they were given an opportunity to talk about their problems, to listen to someone's story, and to take the perspective of another person. In a similar study, McCormick (1988) found that the troublemakers were just as eager to learn about the mediation process and were just as expert as peer mediators who were viewed by teachers as well-behaved students.

Conclusion

We have looked at three major forms of peer counselling and support. In Chapters 3 and 4 we describe the contexts in which peer counselling and support services are most likely to flourish. The theme of the following two chapters is the development and implementation of systems which empower young people by giving them opportunities to play an active part in their own school community.

CHAPTER 3

The Context of Peer Counselling

The effective peer counselling service is more likely to thrive in a supportive and proactive environment which overtly values constructive social relationships amongst peers and adults. The context for this is created by the school. This can be achieved by developing the peer counselling service within the framework of a whole-school policy on social relationships within the school and by ensuring that the ethical and moral issues relating to the involvement of peers in counselling their fellow students have been attended to. The policy will relate to general behaviour, bullying, prejudice and harassment as well as to pastoral care. If the peer counselling service develops in an arbitrary and unconnected way, in isolation from any social policy, then its effectiveness is likely to be diminished or haphazard. Without consideration of ethical and moral issues, the service runs the risk of creating more difficulties than solutions. The aim of this chapter is to examine the context of peer counselling and support – factors which should be considered by schools *before* involving peers in supporting other peers.

The nature of whole-school behaviour policies

A whole-school policy is a document which states the aims of the school and describes how these aims will be achieved. Policies inform and shape practice within the school. Whole-school policies are those which have implications for everybody within the school community.

Policies relating to the management of behaviour usually fall into two groups (Thompson and Sharp, 1994). The policies in the first group concern themselves with organisational aspects of behaviour. These kinds of policies are constructed to assist with the smooth running of the school. They therefore aim to promote effective study skills and to regulate movement around the school, punctuality, dress requirements, health and safety issues. The policies in the second group relate more to the development and maintenance of constructive relationships between members of the school community. They specify expectations of interactions between students and staff and are usually firmly based upon a philosophy of equal opportunities. These kinds of policies concern themselves with challenging racism, sexism and bullying behaviour and examine how the social fabric of the school can be enhanced. Both types of policy are important in providing a calm and purposeful educational environment. Those in the second group are particularly important in providing an appropriate framework for a peer counselling service.

The value of whole-school behaviour policies

As we have seen in Chapter 2, the extensive work in Canada on peer counselling (Carr, 1994) indicates that the best settings are those where there is a policy which actually promotes values of cooperation and where there is a commitment to relationships based upon mutuality and trust.

The Elton Report (Elton, 1989) clarified that establishing good behaviour and discipline was dependent upon involving most members of the school community, setting out clear expectations as to what is and is not acceptable, and ensuring a mutual understanding of the principles upon which practice is based. By examining good practice in schools across the country, the report demonstrated that schools could actively promote positive relationships amongst peers and adults.

Recent research into tackling bullying in schools (Smith and Sharp, 1994) has demonstrated that levels of bullying can be significantly reduced by using the process of policy development. Through this process schools can establish a clear definition of appropriate and inappropriate behaviour and provide guidelines for consistent preventative and reactive action. These studies demonstrate that strategies, such as peer counselling, which are implemented as part of a whole-school policy are more likely to have an impact upon behaviour than those which are not. Without the framework of a whole-school policy, the impact of any intervention will be restricted to a small subsection of the school community and is unlikely to be maintained over time. Without a policy to back it up, the peer counselling service will depend upon the goodwill of committed staff and children. As these individuals leave or develop new interests, the peer counselling service will wane.

The process of establishing a whole-school behaviour policy

The process of establishing a whole-school policy can be described in terms of four stages. These involve:

- identifying the need for policy development;
- agreeing what the policy should consist of;
- putting the policy into practice;
- ensuring the policy is effective.

Identifying the need for a whole-school policy

A whole-school policy is one which is implemented throughout the school and which therefore usually has implications for everybody within the school community. This typically means that a large number of people will need to be involved in the process of policy development. A significant amount of effort will be required both to complete this process and to ensure that the policy is firmly established. Motivation to be involved in this process will encourage individuals to maintain effort. This may be particularly important if some members of the school community do not fully understand how successful learning relates to the maintenance of constructive relationships. Before embarking on the process of policy development, the role of senior management will be to clarify why such a policy is needed and how the practice of individuals will benefit from putting effort into establishing it.

Agreeing what the policy should consist of

To achieve consensus about policy content there will need to be some discussion and debate about the purpose of the policy as well as the range of strategies which could be implemented. This will require opportunities for exploration and sharing of values and attitudes relating to social relationships and behaviour as well as information exchange and consultation. The process of agreeing what the policy should consist of can be managed by careful timetabling and planning. The school calendar includes times for meetings with staff, parents and governors. Opportunities for awareness raising and discussion can be included in these meetings. The curriculum provides a forum for debate with students.

Some kinds of policy can be developed by a small group of staff and then communicated more widely within the school community. Policies which relate to social behaviour, however, depend upon more extensive opportunities for discussion and a greater degree of involvement to ensure implementation. In examining closely the important aspects of policy development, participation of all staff, students and families has been recognised as vital. As part of the DFE-funded Sheffield anti-bullying project directed by Peter Smith, Thompson and Sharp (1994) looked at the role of whole-school policies in reducing levels of bullying in schools. They found that the largest reductions in levels of reported bullying occurred in schools where the highest proportion of staff had actively participated in the development process. Schools which extended the consultation process to include students and families had a greater impact upon student perceptions of school effectiveness in tackling bullying and increased the likelihood of students telling a member of staff if they were being bullied. During interviews with teachers who had been involved in the anti-bullying project, 75 per cent of those interviewed referred to improvements in student and staff attitude and behaviour following involvement in discussion about the nature of the problem and consultation about anti-bullying approaches.

The process of consultation emphasises collective responsibility for the maintenance of constructive relationships. This responsibility is shared equally by both adults and young people within the context of school. It affects how the curriculum is delivered, how communications within the school are managed, how individuals and groups relate to each other within the classroom, during lunch and breaktimes and when moving around the school. Pro-social behaviour cannot be easily enforced by adults alone. Individuals and groups within the school need to be motivated to be considerate of others and to manage both close and occasional relationships in a constructive manner. The policy will need to describe when and how members of the school community will be shown how to manage their relationships in a constructive manner as well as including strategies for responding when relationships break down. One strategy could be to approach the peer counselling service for support.

Putting the policy into practice

If the aim of the policy is to improve the way in which children and adults relate to each other, it may be necessary specifically to teach both children and adults how to manage their relationships more effectively. Implementation of the policy will depend upon adults and young people being familiar with the broad range of skills needed to achieve this.

Kreidler (1984) describes five core qualities needed to help maintain constructive relationships within a school. These qualities are:

1 Cooperation: Individuals learn to work together, to trust, to help and share with each other.
2 Communication: Individuals learn to observe more carefully, communicate needs and wants and listen sensitively.
3 Positive emotional expression: Individuals learn to express their feelings (including anger, fear and frustration) in ways which are not aggressive or destructive.
4 Appreciation of diversity: Individuals learn to respect and appreciate difference and similarities and to understand how prejudice works.
5 Conflict resolution: Individuals learn the skills of responding creatively to conflict.

An effective policy will identify ways in which these core qualities will be promoted and taught. Research suggests that unless taught otherwise, children tend to resolve conflict by using aggression, bullying or avoidance (DeCecco and Richards,1974). When developing the whole-school policy, staff need to recognise that neither teachers nor children always come to school already equipped to handle more difficult aspects of relationships. They need to be taught how to do this. The policy in practice will also need to promote an understanding of conflict as a problem to be solved rather than a contest to be won. To be able to resolve conflict constructively, individuals need to understand what conflict is and how it can lead to either positive or negative outcomes. They also need to recognise the value of a positive outcome for themselves and for others so that they will be willing to implement constructive conflict resolution strategies. Finally, they need to learn and practise the basic skills involved in constructive conflict management: active listening and assertiveness. Direct teaching of these essential communication skills helps adults and children to manage their relationships with others. Outbursts of aggressive behaviour, bullying and harassment often reflect ignorance of other ways of expressing anger, fear or frustration, or a lack of experience in negotiation or discussion.

Both the curriculum and staff development opportunities can be used to enhance the repertoire of relationship management skills and to promote expectations of positive behaviour. Actually putting the policy into practice will depend upon adults feeling competent to implement the policy, and on regular reminders to the whole community of what the policy consists of and what its implications are for behaviour.

Ensuring the policy is effective

Establishing the effectiveness of the policy in practice will depend upon monitoring procedures being established and implemented. Indicators of a successful policy can be based upon three different aspects of implementation:

- familiarity with the policy by those who should be operating it;
- effects of the policy upon adult and student behaviour;
- staff, student and parent satisfaction with the policy in practice.

Gathering data about the quality of social relationships on a regular basis can be a rewarding way of monitoring the effectiveness of a whole-school policy in practice. Annual administration of a student, staff and family questionnaire can yield interesting information about the social fabric of the school. Through such questionnaires schools can monitor changes in the nature and extent of aggressive and cooperative behaviour, student attitudes towards each other, perceived effectiveness of the policy in practice. Individual student plans developed with students who frequently experience difficulties with managing relationships constructively can also be monitored to identify how successfully they have achieved agreed goals. Information from reports of specific incidents where relationships have broken down and where staff have been involved can be collated to provide information about trends in student behaviour and effectiveness of staff responses. Feedback of information collected via monitoring helps to maintain motivation for continued implementation, inform necessary changes in practice and target good practice as well as problem areas.

The peer counselling service and the whole-school behaviour policy

The peer counselling service can be considered as one aspect of implementing a whole-school behaviour policy. Including references to the service within the policy conveys a number of messages about the way the service is viewed by the school. The peer counselling service becomes integrated into the range of preventative strategies used by the school. It is seen, by both students and staff, as being as important as other kinds of strategy – many of which may emphasise the adult rather than the student role. The nature of the service reinforces the value of discussing problems and difficulties with peers or adults. By involving students in the resolution of difficulties, the school demonstrates its recognition of the ways in which young people can contribute effectively to the problem-solving process and do have a positive contribution to make to the social welfare of the school. By introducing peer counselling services, schools place trust in the abilities of their students. The peer counselling service also acknowledges the rights of students to choose who they discuss their concerns with. Inclusion of the service in the policy also ensures that the service is linked to other preventative and response strategies. In this way it is protected from becoming an alternative to a supportive, listening staff. In a practical sense, its inclusion ensures that time and consideration will be given to training and supporting youngsters and monitoring the quality of service delivery.

Ethical issues in peer counselling

> Sooner or later every person involved in helping others must face and deal with the complex issues implied by the following questions: Can I be a friend to my counsellees? Can I be a counsellor to my friends? (Kennedy and Charles, 1977)

Ethical dilemmas relating to counselling relationships will always emerge. For this reason, professional counsellors usually adhere to a code of conduct which guides their practice. Such codes will address issues of relationship boundaries, confidentiality, the need for supervision. Schools who are setting up a peer counselling service will need to address these issues too.

The benefits of peer counselling in schools are discussed at length in other chapters and it is clear that the gains made by individual children and the school as a whole are considerable. At the same time, we argue that it is impossible not to bring moral considerations into peer counselling since many of the issues addressed in peer counselling concern moral decisions: "I'm so unhappy at this new school. What should I do?"; "I'm being bullied by Jo. How can I cope? Should I get a gang on to him?"; "My parents have split up and each one wants me to take their side. What should I do?"; "I know that my best friend's boyfriend is going out with someone else. Should I tell her?"

The potential for moral and ethical difficulties arising through the peer counselling service will always exist and it is important that any school which is considering setting up such a service thinks carefully about the ethical issues of running such a service and ensures that safety checks are in place before the service begins to operate. However much responsibility is shared with students, the senior managers and teaching staff of the school remain ultimately accountable for all that takes place during the school day. This section aims to explore some of the difficulties which may arise when running a service and to discuss some of the preventative strategies which could be helpful.

The boundaries of the counselling relationship

The boundaries of the counselling relationship can be defined along two dimensions. Firstly there are boundaries which relate to the nature of the peer counsellor role and the client–counsellor relationship within and beyond the counselling situation. Secondly, there are boundaries concerning the type of difficulty which peer counsellors are able to work with. Problems can arise when the boundaries of the counselling relationship are unclear, and schools who are planning to introduce a peer counselling service need to be explicit about the purpose of the service and consequently the limitations of the peer counselling role and client–counsellor relationship.

The role of peer counsellor

In our work we have deliberately restricted the role of the peer counsellors to that of active listener and facilitator, whether in one-to-one support, small group support or conflict resolution in the case of a dispute. The young people who become peer counsellors are not full-time professional counsellors or psychotherapists. Their role is simply to provide a safe opportunity for another young person to share their concerns, to be taken seriously and to explore their own solutions to the difficulties they are encountering. This neutral but helpful role is carefully limited to maximise its potential for success and this can be difficult for young people to accept. Most of the young people who volunteer to train as peer counsellors are motivated to do so out of a desire to help. They want to make things better for others, to prevent their peers from making mistakes or from feeling hurt. They often want to protect their peers in a way perhaps they would like to have been protected themselves. The deliberately restricted role of listener or facilitator can at the outset feel frustratingly narrow for the young person until their experience teaches them how useful being actively listened to can be. As described elsewhere in this book, the role of peer counsellors or supporters can also extend to mediation work and befriending. This has been achieved successfully in many schools. The need to be clear about the role and responsibilities of the young people and the school staff remains, whatever the function of the service.

Peer counsellors are not advice givers. It is worthwhile investing time in exploring with young people how advice giving can be unhelpful to their peers. As advice givers peer counsellors are not acting as supportive listeners and they cannot be certain they are giving the right information. They may frustrate their client or misguide them. The potential harm of the latter outcome should not be underestimated. If, as a result of a piece of advice given in a counselling situation, a young person comes to physical or emotional harm, who is to blame? The school will be accountable and the negative impact on the young person offering that advice could be significant. By restricting the role of counsellor to helping the client explore their own solutions, the counsellor, the client and the school are reasonably protected. In a befriending role it can sometimes be appropriate to give advice. The nature of this advice is usually agreed beforehand. For example, a student who regularly calls out in class may have a befriending relationship with another student which involves the peer supporter saying, "Put your hand up, don't call out!" as and when appropriate. Where advice giving is a part of peer support, it should be emphasised that although it may be part of the role of the peer supporter to give advice, it is not their responsibility to make sure their advice is followed. The student in the example above may choose to ignore their peer and continue to interrupt. That is their choice and their responsibility.

The client–counsellor relationship

The peer counsellors should be able to recognise and accept that their relationship with their client is restricted to the time they spend in the counselling situation. It is not appropriate for them to be overly supportive of that young person or to refer to their counselling relationship at other times. This can be difficult if the peer counsellor and client are in the same class or year group. If, as is often the case, the problem brought to the counselling situation relates to a relationship difficulty with another peer, the counsellor must also be able to carry on their day-to-day involvement in school life without being affected by this knowledge. This disengagement outside the counselling situation can create dilemmas for the peer counsellor which should be addressed through supervision and support.

Peer counsellors are not advocates for their clients. If peer counsellors are tempted to become advocates for their clients they overstep the boundaries of client–counsellor relationship and take their role of counsellor beyond the counselling situation. Advocacy reinforces the helplessness of the client by denying them the opportunity to implement their own solutions. It also makes confidentiality difficult to maintain. In a worst-case scenario it can lead to peer counsellors acting as vigilantes seeking to avenge their clients or resolve situations by putting their own safety at risk.

As a peer intervention, befriending can provide a powerful framework for support (see Chapter 6 for an account of the Circle of Friends process). However, if not handled carefully, befriending can promote overdependency by the client upon the counsellor and can encourage unequal relationships marked by obligation. Friendship, befriending and counselling relationships are all potentially intimate, but there are important differences between them, and the peer counsellors need to be able to identify these differences and behave accordingly. Most professional counselling bodies provide an ethical code of practice which clearly recognises that personal relationships and professional relationships should be kept separate. Within a peer counselling or supporting setting the value of such ethical principles should be discussed. Natural friendships may arise or already exist between counsellor and client. Such relationships can be built upon through befriending but may be disadvantageous in a counselling relationship. The impact of natural friendships on peer support should be explored during initial training and also during supervision.

The nature of problems explored within the peer counselling situation

As we have seen, pastoral care services in schools are often greatly over-stretched. The moral dilemma faced by teachers in a pastoral role is that too often they lack the time or resources to deal as effectively as they would like with the problems brought to their attention. By changing role from direct provider of a service to manager of a peer-led support team, these teachers may well increase their effectiveness. But this transition must be done with care. It is not about "off-loading" insoluble problems on to peer counsellors. Rather the role of initiator and manager of a peer support service provides a significant opportunity to empower young people and help them to practise roles and responsibilities in their own school community. It involves the recognition of what young people have the potential to do within the safe supportive context of appropriate training and on-going supervision.

Whilst young people are competent to deal with a wide range of difficulties, there are some aspects of children's lives which should be referred directly to adults because of legal implications. We advise that peer counsellors do not undertake to support peers who are being physically or sexually abused or harmed in any way. Training and supervision must address the possibility of these issues being brought to the peer counsellor and the young people should be coached in ways of responding. It is up to each school to think carefully about the range of issues the counselling service can work with. The training and supervision offered to peer counsellors may then need to address each of these issues to ensure that the counsellors have a broader understanding of the nature of the problem. Common issues brought to peer counselling services include relationship difficulties (with peers and with teachers), bullying and harassment, study problems, family problems (siblings, divorce, discipline), peer pressure, concerns about physical development. Other issues might include bereavement (of friend, relative or pet), drug-related difficulties, sexual relationships, financial hardship.

Where the teachers share responsibility for these sensitive issues and provide appropriate training, updating and supervision, the outcomes can be very encouraging. Adults involved in the field of peer counselling often express surprise at the resourcefulness of the young helpers. In addition, adults and students involved in the process often end up with quite different views of one another based on mutual trust. The young people are much more likely to see the teachers involved in training and supervision as genuine educators who value them personally. The atmosphere during training and supervision sessions becomes one of a community of helpers based on democratic rather than hierarchical principles. So the experience of engaging in peer counselling not only helps peers in distress; it also facilitates change in the values of those involved.

Similarly, the experience of taking part in peer counselling provides the opportunity for changes in the perceptions which young people have of one another. For example, they have the chance to develop greater tolerance for difference, a growing respect for others and a generally more accepting, non-judgemental attitude towards peers. This is, of course, an on-going process which does not happen immediately. Partly it arises out of the experience of empathising with the feelings of another person. Partly too it arises out of the self-reflective stance which is encouraged during training and supervision. In the early stages, the peer counsellors may think that they know what it feels like to be the client in distress, and the evidence we have suggests that young people are in some significant ways in a stronger position to be able to enter into the experience of someone in their age-group. However, the experience of engaging in a counselling relationship also teaches humility. There is always the danger of underestimating the distress of the other. Personal values and cultural background may get in the way of being helpful. The behaviour and attitudes of the client may challenge the beliefs of the helper – yet disapproval of the client is not helpful.

Peer counsellors need to be given opportunities for training and supervision to become sensitive to the moral conflicts which their clients are experiencing. They need to be helped to become aware of the values and judgements which they bring to the counselling situation. This does not mean that the peer counsellor should learn to be morally neutral – even if this were possible. On the contrary, the peer counsellor needs to learn to be in tune with his or her own values and to be in the process of understanding what they are and where they come from.

Here is an example of a situation where the counsellor has to understand the wider moral context as well as the immediate concerns of the client. Shani is upset because she is not allowed out in the evenings by her parents. Her brother is allowed far more freedom. She feels that this is unfair and she is resentful. The peer counsellor must understand that this rule against which Shani rebels is part of a cultural tradition. It is not enough for the peer counsellor to try to empower Shani to challenge her parents without seeing the parents' behaviour in a wider cultural context.

The nature of confidentiality

Within a professional counselling relationship which involves adults counselling adults, confidentiality can be assured. Within a school situation where adults or peers are counselling young people, absolute confidentiality is rarely achievable and not necessarily appropriate. Legally, schools are bound to take action if a child or young person discloses abuse; therefore we can never promise secrecy. The 1989 Children Act prescribes limits to confidentiality. If abuse or significant harm is suspected, adults must pass on their concerns about the student to the appropriate social services department. So where does this leave the peer counsellor? The peer counsellor can agree that they will not discuss the content of the counselling session or the identity of the client with anybody outside the service, but they should report regularly to a named member of staff. How far can peer counsellors, however well-meaning, be trusted to address in a sensitive and responsible way the complexities of the problems which their peers are likely to be experiencing? Even if they recognise the difficulties, do they have the skill to clarify them and discuss them with their clients? What happens if they encounter behaviour which is pathological? It is important for the teacher responsible to provide regular opportunities for peer counsellors to share concerns with their group and to offer supervision for issues as they arise.

The school does need to monitor how the service is being used to provide an essential safety net for picking up problem cases which should be being dealt with by teaching staff, as illustrated here by a young person talking to a peer counsellor in one of the Peer Counselling Project schools:

> ... things were getting really out of hand ... the client had become involved in some really nasty stuff with gangs and drugs and knives. I kept on thinking that I could handle it by myself ... in a way I think I was trying to prove something to myself by holding on to it ... I knew that I should be talking to Mrs B about it – that it was bigger than I could handle ... I started having nightmares about the client dying and it would be my fault for not telling someone. It was a relief when Mrs B came to see me ... she had been reading my case notes ... if she hadn't I don't know where it would have ended.

It can be helpful to ensure that each peer counsellor meets regularly with a named member of staff to discuss all current cases. In this way, the school supports the counsellor and ensures that the counsellor is working within the agreed boundaries of the service. This kind of case discussion can occur individually or within the context of a supervision group which includes other peer counsellors.

Confidentiality extends to record keeping and note taking. Keeping a brief record of the age, gender and race of the client can provide useful data for monitoring who is using the service. This can help in making adjustments in how the service is organised or advertised. Recording the nature of the case, the dates of visits and the outcome helps the counsellor to keep a record for reference of work undertaken and enables the named staff member to overview how the service is being used. Whether the counsellor records the name of the client or not is something which the school will have to decide. Not recording the name protects the identity of the client. In some circumstances, however, it may be important to know who has used the service and when. This is particularly so if a serious incident occurs which involves a student who has used the service or if the case is referred to a member of staff who might want to know what action had already been taken.

Whatever information is collected, it must be stored carefully and securely but be accessible to the client or the client's parents if requested.

(This also applies to any information stored on computer, which is subject to the Data Protection Act.) Files containing information about clients should not be carried around the school in a counsellor's bag, stored in a student locker or taken home.

The importance of support and supervision

Most professonal counsellors continually reflect upon their practice and establish opportunities of some kind to discuss their work with another counsellor on a regular basis. These opportunities are usually called "supervision". This kind of support is not only helpful for exploring difficult cases but can provide feedback for the counsellor about the effectiveness of their counselling style and the impact of their work upon themselves and their client.

The word "supervision" can have different meanings for different people. Literally, it means "to over-look". People's experiences of supervision will shape their perceptions of what it is and what it might mean. Outside the counselling or clinical setting, supervision is often defined as having one's work checked for accuracy. It therefore becomes a situation where one's work is judged. This can be threatening and anxiety-provoking in individuals and may lead to situations where people avoid sharing pieces of work they are most concerned about or are experiencing difficulty with. We use the term "supervision" to describe a situation whereby a person reflects collaboratively upon different aspects of his or her work with a view to continuing the learning process. Scaife (1993) describes supervision as "a context for co-operation in which the possibility of satisfactory learning is enhanced". Within your school, you may wish to use the word "supervision" or you may choose an alternative word, such as "support", "reflection", "casework discussion".

There are different models of supervision. The one we will explore here is that proposed by Scaife (1993). In her "General Supervision Framework", Scaife describes three different aspects of supervision: role and behaviour of the supervisor; the focus for the supervision; the medium in which the supervision occurs.

The role and behaviour of the supervisor

Supervisors can take on many roles. Scaife identifies three in particular which can be helpful within the supervision situation. The supervisor will use all three at appropriate points in the supervision meeting and must guard against a preference for a particular role which would limit the outcomes of the supervision for the other person.

In the first role, "inform–assess", the supervisor is involved in commenting upon the other person's performance. In this role, the supervisor may be acknowledged as someone who "knows more" than the supervisee. They therefore might give information about a particular aspect of the work or undertake a training role.

Another role the supervisor might undertake is that of "enquirer". In this role the supervisor asks questions and may share their own experiences. This role is based upon joint exploration to which there are no predetermined right answers.

The third role is that of "listen–reflect". This role is based upon active listening and reflection. Through this role the supervisor is able to support the other person in seeing an overview of the work, in understanding the feelings generated by the work and in making it easier for the other to develop their own explanations of any difficulties they may be facing.

A useful activity for a supervisor is to tape a supervision meeting and then analyse the range of roles adopted during the session. In this way, supervisors can check against over-use or under-use of a particular style.

Focus for supervision meetings

The focus for supervision sessions will usually be negotiated. Often, there will be a particular piece of casework or issue that the supervisee wants to explore. In the first few minutes of the session it is helpful for each person to identify their agenda for that meeting. This ensures effective use of time and assists with clarity of purpose for the meeting. In a school setting, where supervision may take place in a group setting and often within a fairly restricted time schedule, this is especially important. Some teachers like to begin each session with each person giving a brief overview of work undertaken since the last meeting. The remainder of the session uses a negotiated agenda with an agreed purpose. Three common questions for the beginning of supervision might be:

"What would you like to explore?"
"What do you hope to gain from this session?"
"How do you think I/the other group members can be most helpful?"

The supervision session may focus on actions and events. This would include exploring specific behaviours and skills used by the peer counsellor. Alternatively, the focus may be knowledge, thinking and planning – linking theory and practice. At other times the focus could be orientated towards feelings and personal qualities, exploring how the peer counsellor expresses their individual style within their work or how a piece of work has affected them.

Scaife points out that, as with role and behaviour, both supervisor and supervisee are likely to have strong personal preferences for focus. The focus needs to be negotiated and agreed and any bias by either party noted and explored.

Medium for supervision sessions

Supervision can occur in a range of different media – it can be based upon verbally reported information, it can be re-enacted through role play, it can be recorded upon tape or video, it can be live.

Reported supervision is most widely used because of its practical ease. This type of supervision involves the supervisee reporting upon work undertaken and therefore is retrospective. This type of supervision is easily manageable and fairly safe as the supervisee has control over the information fed into the supervision meeting. However, information can be lost, forgotten or embellished. Difficult issues may be avoided rather than raised. Within a reported supervision setting, role play can provide a useful method for exploring the situation and examining the different dimensions of the counselling relationships. It can be helpful for the supervisor to take on the role of the counsellor in the first instance, so that the supervisee can experience the counselling situation from the client's perspective. In a group supervision setting, by encouraging the supervisee to direct rather than take part in the re-enactment of the counselling situation, i.e. by choosing others to play the role of client and him/herself, the supervisee can assume a more objective role and actually "observe" the counselling process.

Counselling situations can be recorded, either on audio tape or on video. The client needs to agree to this and confidentiality and security of recorded material should be assured. Recording counselling sessions to explore during supervision ensures accurate material and increases the likelihood of objectivity within the supervision. It allows repeated replay of particular aspects of the work. Kagan and Kagan (1991) developed an approach for use of video material in counselling training called Interpersonal Process Recall (IPR). In IPR, a counselling session is recorded. It is then replayed by the supervisee in the presence of another person, known as the enquirer. The supervisee has control of the video playback and stops the recording at any points s/he chooses. The enquirer then asks a series of questions which aim to enable the supervisee to focus on the feelings generated by the counselling exchange.

Live supervision can be very empowering. It involves the supervisor being present during a counselling session. The role of the supervisor and the purpose of the session should be clearly agreed beforehand with both the supervisee and the client. Sometimes, it may be appropriate for the supervisor to maintain the role of silent observer during the session, with time set aside afterwards for discussion of the session. At other times the supervisee may prefer the supervisor to become an active participant in the session, therefore creating a co-counselling situation. Alternatively, the supervisee might wish the supervisor to participate but only to address comments to him/herself – i.e. not to engage directly with the client or to contribute only on request.

An extension of live supervision is the reflective team. In family therapy it is common to have a counselling session observed by a team of two or three other counsellors, separated from the counselling session by a screen or two-way mirror. Microphones or earphones allow comments or questions on the counselling session to be communicated either one way or both ways. Anderson (1987) describes how helpful it can be to both counsellor and client to listen in on the comments of the reflective team. This can add another dimension to the quality of supervision.

Prioritising support and supervision within the school setting

With all the competing pressures of school life it can be very easy for staff to dismiss supervision as an added extra or luxury item which can be missed out. De Rosenroll (1989) reports that school staff often complain that they spend as much time on training and supervision as they previously spent counselling young people. Supervision is essential for the maintenance and continued development of a quality peer counselling service and therefore does take time. Without supervision a school could be seen as negligent. Here are one teacher's comments on supervision:

> At the outset I didn't realise how important supervision can be – I thought it was some fad and that by monitoring the counsellor's notes I could make sure everything was OK. Before it was so easy to miss out supervision – after all, lunchtimes are so busy! Now, I wouldn't be without it – it's our lifeline and it has helped us to learn more, to extend the service and to avoid some pretty horrendous mistakes. Because of the limitations of time, we have group supervision once a fortnight – it isn't enough, I know. I'm hoping that when

> Mrs X starts working with the service next term we will meet weekly. My advice to anyone starting up is – you've got to have it – miss it out at your peril.

A student describes the benefits of group supervsion:

> The supervision meetings are so helpful ... you learn so much from sharing your own experiences and from hearing others ... you realise that all the worries you have, well, everyone else has them too! To talk about a case you are working on is reassuring ... to check it out with others, to get some new ideas, to stop you getting into bad habits! At first it was a bit scary ... to tell other people what you were doing ... I was afraid I might have done something wrong and people would laugh but it's just not like that ... it's great.

The regular provision of opportunities for supervision can be achieved through planning and organisation at the inception of the service. Such meetings can take place during the school day or after school. Some schools have deliberately chosen to keep one lunchtime a week for group supervision meetings. This can be supplemented by individual supervision sessions on a half-termly basis. Carr (1988) describes a city-wide peer counselling service which placed a particular emphasis on supervision during an extended training period. Young people who trained as peer counsellors received 45 hours of supervised in school work experience as well as 60 hours of training. The supervision included maintenance of personal self-reporting forms and video-taped work. Guttman (1985) also viewed supervision as an extension of the initial training programme. In her work, weekly group meetings included discussion of individual and group counselling activities. In Canadian peer counselling projects the issue of manageability of training, support and supervision has been addressed by encouraging the development of centralised peer counselling initiatives for local networks of schools. This enables peer counsellors from more than one school to come together to receive training and supervision, and shares the burden of time costs over several schools. Such projects do need within-school support but this is less intensive. De Rosenroll (1989) offered an initial training programme, a series of weekly meetings during the first two terms of in-school practice and monthly support meetings from then on. School staff were expected to hold regular in-school meetings to supplement this. Carr (1988) reports on the benefits of a city-wide peer counselling programme in Victoria, Canada. In this project, students from all schools in the city were invited to join in the training programme. Additional benefits included greater accessibility to appropriately trained personnel, to offer training and opportunities for on-going support and consultation for the school staff as as well as the students.

Space, time and resources

The establishment and maintenance of a peer counselling service requires some physical preparation. The service needs a location within the school; time for both students and staff to be involved in training, supervision and day-to-day operation; financial and material resourcing for initial training, advertising and on-going record keeping and storage.

A peer support service will need access to at least one room where privacy can be assured. Classrooms can be used, office-style accommodation is preferable. If staff are willing to provide office space, they must be prepared to stay out of the office whilst it is being used for peer support and counselling. The location of the service within the school is another consideration. The service should be easily accessible whilst offering privacy for users of the service. A room off a busy thoroughfare may not be the best location in some schools. On the other hand, promoting the service as something which all students can and should use unashamedly will encourage the view that peer support is a normal and healthy aspect of school life.

Setting up and running a peer support service does not require major financial investment, other than for training if that cannot be provided in-house. The service will need a small budget for advertising and file maintenance. It does however require a significant investment of time and energy from staff, as this teacher describes:

> Having a counselling service does reduce the number of knocks on the staffroom door during breaks and lunchtimes and it does stop the escalation of problems into major crises. ... however, the time saved there is simply re-invested into maintaining the service ... business meetings ... supervision ... training ... all the bits and pieces that go into running a service like this ... there is never enough time.

Ideally, a group of staff should be involved in supporting the service and they must be prepared to be available at times when the service is in operation as well as providing supervision on a regular basis. Many schools do have pastoral staff who have training in counselling and mediation skills and it makes sense for the service to be part of the pastoral system in the school. In preparing for a peer support service, senior managers will need to identify how staff will be involved in the service and how the service will be housed and resourced.

Summary

The whole-school behaviour policy provides the framework within which the peer counselling service operates. The peer counselling service can provide a medium through which the aims of the policy are met in practice. The process of policy development will affect the extent to which this is achievable. Policy development which is based upon a high level of student and staff participation promotes collective responsibility for the constructive management of relationships.

Ethical issues continually arise through peer counselling relationships. They can arise in relation to the counsellor him or herself, the client or the whole school. Many of these can be predicted, such as the extent to which confidentiality can be maintained, and the boundaries of the client–counsellor relationship. Ways of handling these moral dilemmas can be addressed through training. Other issues will emerge through casework, and an effective support and supervision system will ensure that they are tackled responsibly and effectively. Supervision maintains the quality of a peer counselling service by providing a collaborative context for reflection and learning.

The practicalities of running a service, in terms of time, location and resourcing, need clarification and support from senior management.

CHAPTER 4

Setting Up a Training Programme

In this chapter we will focus on the practicalities of providing training for befriending, peer counselling and mediation. Examples of activities are included for each type, but there are clear overlaps in the training, for example in trust-building, forming the training group, the awareness of the feelings of others and the development of active listening skills. Whatever the training programme you are providing, it should prepare students for the kind of support being offered and should reinforce the notion that learning is a continual process. Once the initial training period is over, we continue to learn through reflection and sharing during supervision. All human beings make mistakes: what is important is to manage them as they happen and to learn from them.

Identifying who should be trained

Whether the school wishes to target a specific group of students (for example, Year 11) or is opening up the possibility of peer counselling/support to all students, some way of selecting who will be involved is required. Some schools choose to accept anybody who applies for the training and then assess ability and aptitude during the training process itself. Other schools prefer to emphasise the responsibility of the role by running a more formalised applications scheme.

In one school, pupils were invited to apply formally in writing, giving details of their reasons for wanting to be involved as well as describing what they could offer to the role (see Box 4.1). Care was taken to ensure that peer counsellors represented all the social and ethnic groups in the school community. It was also felt that there should be a reasonable gender balance, although, as in other peer counselling initiatives, a greater number of girls than boys showed interest in taking part. Successful candidates were interviewed and then included on the training programme.

Box 4.1 A sample application form

XXXX SCHOOL PEER COUNSELLING SERVICE

Application Form

Name .... Age

Tutor Group

Why do you think that you would be a good peer counsellor?

What experiences have you had which might help you to be a peer counsellor?

PLEASE COMPLETE AND RETURN TO MS XXXXXX BY 1ST OCTOBER

I give permission for my son/daughter to be involved in the peer counselling initiative at school.

Signed .... Date

The listening and facilitation skills required by peer counsellors can be taught. At this stage of selection staff will be looking for students who can demonstrate a willingness to help and to act responsibly, ability to build relationships with others, empathy, a sense of commitment. A helpful exercise is to develop a list of criteria for selection which can be applied fairly to all students who apply. Some students who may have behaved inappropriately in the past can contribute very effectively to a peer counselling service.

Training for befriending

In Chapter 6, Gill Taylor describes how to set up a Circle of Friends. Here we will briefly consider whole-class activities which will build relationships, increase trust and enhance communications.

Trust-building exercises

Zoom

The whole class stands in a circle. The student who starts says "zoom" to the person on their right, turning their head towards that person. That person turns their head to the left while being spoken to and turns their head to the right whilst saying "zoom" to the next person in the circle. "Zoom" is passed round the circle, going faster and faster. Reverse direction/use names instead of "zoom".

Soundless waves

The whole class stands in a circle. The trainer explains that the circle is like a space ship. In outer space there is no atmosphere to carry sound waves so we communicate through waves of motion. The student who starts makes a shape or combination of arm, leg and body movement and holds it. The person to their left copies the movement and holds it. The movement passes round the circle in this way, getting faster and faster.

Rhythm clap

The whole class sits in a circle. Everyone closes their eyes. Each person claps or taps out any rhythm of their own choosing but listens carefully to the rest of the group. Gradually the group will develop a single rhythm with harmonising variations. Do not tell the students this, simply let it happen. Points for discussion afterwards may include:

- Did I still have a sense of my own individuality while becoming part of the group pattern of sound?
- In what other areas of my life might I experience similar feelings?

Synchronised movement

Everyone stands in their own space, not too near anyone else. On the signal of one clap everyone starts to move around the classroom; encourage people to go in different directions without bumping into anyone. At the second clap everyone becomes absolutely motionless. Practise this so that everyone starts and stops as quickly as possible. Repeat this exercise but without the trainer giving start and stop signals. How quickly can the whole class begin to synchronise their own movements?

Sound location

Prepare pairs of cards with the name of a sound written on each card, e.g. whizz, buzz, sssss etc. Give out one card to each student and ask them to read the word on the card but not to tell it to anyone. Each student closes their eyes and begins to move gently around the room, calling out their sound. They have to locate the student with the same sound as themselves.

Leaning circle

The whole class stands in a circle and is numbered off by twos (one, two, one, two etc.). Ones face toward the centre of the circle, twos face outwards. Everyone grasps the people on either side firmly by the wrists and places their feet together. On the count of three everyone leans back. On the next count of three, everyone leans inwards.

Sitting circle

The whole class stands in a circle. Everyone moves inwards until shoulders are touching. They turn to the right so each person is facing the back of their neighbour. On the count of three, participants bend their knees and lower themselves on to the knees of the person behind. Initially some minor adjustments may need to be made to positioning so everyone is aligned. When the sitting circle is stable everyone can wave their hands in the air. Points for discussion include: what stopped us from falling down? In what other ways could friends support you?

Feeling circle

The whole class sits in a circle. Everybody closes their eyes and thinks about how they are feeling. In turn round the circle, each person completes the sentence, "I feel ...".

Feedback circle

The whole class sits in a circle. Everybody closes their eyes and thinks about someone in the class whom they do not usually spend much time with. They note one positive thing about that person. In turn around the circle, each person completes the sentence, "Today, I have noticed that (other student's name) ... ".

Helping circle

The whole class sits in a circle. Each person closes their eyes and thinks about things they find very hard, to do with school work, behaviour or relationships. Give some examples such as "losing my temper", "joining in with a game", "understanding maths", "listening to the teacher". In turn round the circle, each person completes the sentence, "I would like some help with ...". The trainer notes these down. Once everybody has had a turn, the class discuss how they will help each other.

Ways of helping

Supporting peers and befriending can be immensely rewarding for all concerned. However, it can also be patronising, humiliating and annoying. Practise different phrases and tones of voice through role play. Ask students to evaluate how helpful or unhelpful they might be.

A training course for peer counselling

The essence of peer counselling is good listening – refraining from interrupting, paraphrasing, being comfortable with silence and emotion, understanding body language and social distancing. The aim of the counselling is to enable the client to explore and define the problem they are experiencing and to help them to arrive at a new understanding of the problem or to develop a solution to the difficulty they are encountering.

Training should be done by an experienced counsellor who is willing to work in close cooperation with the teaching staff at the school. Staff within the school who are appropriately trained could help with this, as could support agencies for the school, such as educational psychologists, behavioural support teams or educational welfare officers. We found Egan (1990) and Inskipp (1986) particularly useful in designing our training programme.

Initial training can take place in a series of short sessions of 45 minutes, or more intensively in a series of half- or whole-day workshops. The following exercises cover the concepts of:

- building trust
- understanding the qualities of the peer counsellor
- developing active listening skills
- dealing with difficult emotions
- developing a vocabulary of feelings

Trust-building exercises

If the students feel they can trust each other they will feel more confident in experimenting with new skills and in sharing their experiences as they work as counsellors. Although the students who have applied may be in the same class or year group, they may not necessarily know each other very well. We begin with some examples of ice-breakers.

The daisy chain

Participants sit in a circle. The first person introduces herself – for example, "I'm Claire." The person sitting beside Claire says, "This is Claire and I am John." The person beside John says, "This is Claire; this is John and I am Michael." The introductions go round the circle, with the list of names getting longer, until the last person introduces everyone! The group is encouraged to help people when, as some inevitably do, they forget a name.

Sylvester

Participants sit in a circle. The leader produces a soft toy and explains that he will throw "Sylvester" to a member of the group and call out that person's name. The recipient in turn is invited to throw Sylvester to another member of the group, again calling that person's name. The game ends when everybody's name has been called at least once.

Modelling

Participants sit in a circle. In turn, each group member "models" in imaginary clay an appropriate present for the person on their left. (They will have learned something about the person during self-introduction in pairs.) The imaginary clay model is "handed over" and "received".

Self-introduction

Participants work in pairs. Each person takes it in turn to tell their partner three distinctive things about themselves. The pairs re-form in a circle.

Each person introduces their partner to the whole group, for example, "This is Stacey and she likes ... "

Giant knot

All participants stand in a circle. Everyone raises their left hand above their head and extends their right hand out in front of them. They close their eyes and walk slowly into the centre or the circle. Each person joins their raised hand with someone else's raised hand and their extended hand with a different person's extended hand. When both hands are linked with other people, the participant may open their eyes. Through doing this, the group will have formed a knot of people. The group must then try to untangle themselves whilst still holding hands. Once untangled the whole group will be in a circle with hands held!

Blindfold guiding

Participants work in pairs. One person is blindfolded, the other acts as their guide and directs them verbally around the room.

Facilitating the qualities of the peer counsellor

The essential quality of the peer counsellor is being able to relate to others easily, and this includes warmth, genuineness, acceptance and empathy. Here are some examples of activities which will help to develop these qualities.

Sharing

Participants sit in a circle. The leader invites each member of the group to think of something which they have never confided to anyone before. It may be something they have done or experienced which they feel ashamed of. It may be something so personal that they feel reluctant to talk about it for fear of being ridiculed. It may refer to a very deep feeling. Give the group time to think about this issue. *Stress that they will not be asked to share it with anyone on this occasion.* The task is to look round the group and think if there is anyone in the circle in whom they might confide. *They do not reveal the name of the person.* The group facilitator then asks each person to think about why they might have chosen that person to share their secret with, and what that person's special qualities are. The facilitator lists these qualities on a flip chart, highlighting the fact that they are all present in the group, for example by saying, "You have just described the qualities of a peer counsellor ... and they are present in this group." Attributes which are often mentioned include trust, friendship, listening skill, no put-downs, the capacity to respect a confidence (see Figure 4.1). These are the qualities which will be developed in the course of training.

Figure 4.1 Qualities of the peer counsellor

Establishing a helping relationship

The facilitator asks students to brainstorm ways of forming a helping relationship by asking, for example, "From your own experience, what kind of things can people do to help and support one another?" This activity usually raises the issue of giving advice. The facilitator stresses that the peer counsellor's role is to facilitate the process of problem solving by the clients. Peer counsellors do not usually give advice or solve problems for others. They are there in the role of a helping, responsive and sympathetic listener.

Listening skills

Listening skills are the key to providing counselling help. In usual relationships our conversations include turn taking, sharing of experiences, advice giving, story telling, interruptions and digressions. A counselling conversation is different. In a counselling conversation the counsellor is concentrating entirely upon the client's situation. The counsellor listens very attentively, without interrupting or giving advice. Every so often the counsellor will summarise what the client has said and check that s/he has understood correctly. This "reflecting back" of what the client has said can help the client him or herself to clarify the nature of the problem and to identify possible solutions. This type of listening is often called "active listening". Active listening combines two sets of skills: attending and reflecting.

Attending requires the listener to employ appropriate non-verbal behaviour by maintaining an open and attentive posture, through effective eye contact and by sitting near to the other person but without crowding him or her. By giving appropriate cues to the other person, the active listener helps him or her to begin and continue to talk. This will involve giving minimal encouragers such as "Mmm", open questioning and by staying silent when the other person pauses.

Reflecting involves seeking clarification of what has been said, giving responses which summarise both the feelings and factual content expressed by the other person, paraphrasing and summarising. Active listening avoids making judgements, excessive questioning, offering solutions or advice, reassuring or changing the subject.

The following activities aim to enable the students to experience and develop different kinds of attentive behaviour.

Mirroring. Participants (A and B) work in pairs and sit or stand facing each other. A makes a movement; B mirrors it exactly. They do this for two minutes, then reverse roles.

Reflecting back 1. Again, participants work in pairs. A makes a statement about something which is emotionally arousing, for example "I am feeling sad today." B reflects the statement back: "You are feeling sad today." A makes a second statement; B reflects it back. The process is repeated a third time. Without any discussion, A and B switch roles and repeat the process. They then discuss the experience with one another. Finally, in the circle the whole group discusses the issues which have arisen.

Reflecting back 2. The participants work in threes. Each person in turn talks for one minute about an aspect of their life which they like – for example, "something I enjoy doing", "something positive which happened this week" or "something that made me happy". When all three have made their statements, they take it in turn to repeat as accurately as they can what the other said, but without parroting. At the end, the three discuss this experience and how they felt about it.

Reflecting back with an observer. There are three roles in this exercise – client, counsellor and observer. The client talks for three minutes (the observer keeps time) about something which made them upset, for example "I felt very sad when ...", "I became angry when ..." or "a very annoying thing which happened was ..." The counsellor reflects back as accurately as possible, and without comment, what the client has said. The observer stays silent but makes notes on the quality of the interaction, using the following checklist:

- eye contact
- gestures
- body position
- facial expression
- tone of voice

and considering the following questions:

1 What messages were conveyed by the counsellor's eyes, gestures, body position, facial expression?
2 How appropriate was the voice of the counsellor?
3 How interested did the counsellor appear in the client's problem? What evidence have you for this opinion?

Debriefing takes place among all three at the end. We recommend that feedback is given first by the observer, second by the client and finally by the counsellor. This feedback is followed by general discussion of any issues which have arisen. The roles are rotated until each person has experienced all three.

Paraphrasing. Paraphrasing involves making brief, specific and concrete responses which summarise the key elements of the other person's statements. Participants work in pairs in the roles of client and counsellor. The client makes a statement about something which has aroused feelings. The counsellor paraphrases this statement by saying, "What you seem to be saying is ..." The counsellor takes care not to interpret what the client has said but simply re-phrases using different words. This is repeated twice more before the roles are reversed. The pair then discuss the experience with one another.

Responding to emotion

The young people who use the counselling service are likely to express strong feelings of anger, resentment, distress, revenge etc. Students who are going to be counsellors need to be comfortable with the expression of emotion and allow the other person to express these.

Developing a vocabulary of feelings. Working in a small group, participants brainstorm words which capture nuances of emotion. They find words to express anger, happiness, sadness, guilt, depression, and other feeling states.

Dealing with difficult feelings. Participants work in pairs, as client and counsellor. The client talks about feelings which make him or her feel uncomfortable – for example, jealousy, anger, spitefulness, malice. (Focus on one feeling at a time.) The counsellor listens and then summarises what the client has said. The two then reverse roles. A general discussion then follows on "feelings which are hard to talk about".

Developing a solution. Often simply through having the opportunity to be listened to and to have the account of the problem reflected back through paraphrasing, the client will have begun to formulate their own solutions. This process can be facilitated further by prompts given by the counsellor. Such prompts may include phrases such as:

"So what do you feel you need to change in this situation?"
"What things do you feel you could be doing differently?"
"How could this situation/relationship be improved?"
"What needs to happen?"

The integration of counselling skills

Participants work in pairs, as client and counsellor. The client chooses a role card (see Box 4.2 for some examples) and becomes familiar with the scenario. Then the counsellor, using the skills which have been learned, helps the client to explore the problem. The client allows opportunities for the counsellor to intervene with helpful responses. The counsellor summarises what the client has said and ends the interview.

Box 4.2 Example role cards: bullying situations

You normally hang around with two other friends. You have known one of them since you were at primary school. Recently both of them have been deliberately ignoring you and leaving you out. Yesterday you found out that they have been telling the rest of the class all sorts of nasty stories about you. Some of the things they have said are true and are things you trusted your primary school friend to keep secret.

A group of older pupils keep on hassling you as you walk along the corridors. Each time you pass them they push into you and call you names. Once you met them in the toilets and they held your head under the tap. You are terrified of them. You would like to change school but your parents won't let you. Once or twice you have missed school to avoid them.

In mathematics lessons the teacher arranges the seating. She has made you sit beside someone you don't like very much. This pupil keeps stabbing you in the leg with a pencil. You have got quite a cut there now. The other pupil threatens to beat you up if you tell a teacher.

Another pupil in your form knows that you have skipped off school once or twice. She/he has threatened that unless you miss school to go into town with him or her, s/he will tell your form tutor that you missed school earlier.

Two pupils in your class keep asking you to give them money. They have told you that if you don't give them some money by next Friday they will beat you up. They are very tough and you have heard rumours that they carry knives.

You have recently joined the school. You started half way through the term and feel very lonely. Your accent is slightly different from the other pupils and whenever you try to make friends with anyone you are teased about the way you speak. Now you are frightened to talk to anyone in case they make fun of you.

The client then gives the counsellor some feedback on the extent to which responses were helpful. Questions to explore might include:

Was it helpful?

Did I feel understood?

Did the counsellor listen?

Did I feel that I was accepted?

Did the counsellor move too quickly to a solution?

The roles are then reversed and, using a different role card, the process is repeated. Give students plentiful opportunities for practising through role play.

Variations

Taking the roles of client, counsellor and observer, participants work on one of the role card situations. Feedback is given in order – observer, client and counsellor. Finally the counsellor summarises what he or she has learned from the experience. The roles are rotated. Each role card situation is explored for around three minutes.

Brief the student playing the client to express very strong emotions.

In whole-group discussion, discuss the kinds of counselling situations students are most anxious about. Role-play these situations and explore different ways of responding to them.

"What if ...?" sessions

"What if ...?" sessions enable students to express their anxieties and fears about being a peer counsellor and therefore provide an opportunity for the training sessions to address these. Ask participants to work in pairs and ask them to spend ten minutes talking about aspects of being a counsellor that really worry them. Bring participants back into a circle. Each person completes the sentence "What if ...?" or "How do you ...?". The trainer notes these down. Each concern and question is addressed either through discussion or through role play. Here are some examples of anxieties raised by students during one "What if ...?" session:

- **Forming the client–counsellor relationship**

How do you introduce yourself?

How do you prompt people to begin to speak?

What if the person won't speak?

- **The client–counsellor relationship**

What happens if the client doesn't think you are good enough?

What happens if the client has a disability?

When do you give advice?
What happens if your client laughs at you?
When is it right to bring in your own experience?
What if there is no solution?
What if you laugh when someone is telling bad news?
What if someone gets very emotional? Do you comfort them?
What if someone gets very angry?
What if the client gets stressed and hits out?
What if you think they are hoaxing?

- **Roles and responsibilities**

When do you break confidentiality?
When do you decide to tell a teacher?
What if the counsellors are bullied because they are peer counsellors?
What should you do if you see a client being bullied around school? Should you intervene?
What if someone comes to you and it is about a friend of yours?
What if they tell you the name of the bully?
What if they bring in serious problems from home?
What if it is a teacher who is causing the problem?

- **Advertising the service**

How do you get people to come to you?
What if no one comes?
How do you design posters?

Knowledge of problem areas

Provide some factual information for students about subjects which may come up during counselling. Subjects brought to counsellors commonly include: bullying, relationship difficulties, family arguments, divorce, study skills. They may also encounter students who are having difficulties with a wide range of other areas such as drug or alcohol abuse, sexual relationships, personal hygiene, bedwetting, bereavement or illness. Counsellors may be helped by knowing some facts about the nature and extent of these problems and how they might commonly affect individuals.

Box 4.3 gives an example of the sequence an introductory workshop might follow.

Box 4.3 Introductory workshop

Introduction and welcome What is bullying? What is counselling? How can counselling help people who are being bullied?
Getting to know one another Daisy chain Sylvester The qualities of a peer counsellor
Some basic skills Mirroring Active listening Reflecting back Group share: issues arising
Break
Skills continued Reflecting back with an observer
Silence 2 minutes of reflection followed by any sharing
End

Training for mediation and conflict resolution

In offering training in mediation and conflict resolution, the students will be building upon the listening and facilitating skills already described above and adding to these a step-by-step process which assists two or more people who are in conflict or who have experienced a breakdown of relationships to agree a mutually acceptable solution. In this section, we will describe that process.

Key facts

There are three key facts about conflict and disagreement which any person engaging in mediation or conflict resolution needs to understand.

Firstly, individuals need to know that conflict is not bad. Students may have experienced mainly negative attitudes about conflict: that it causes pain, fear and anger, spoils relationships etc. These negative views are the results of messages about conflict such as "Nice girls don't fight", "Don't get mad, get even", or "If you can't say anything nice, don't say anything at all". If we are to work constructively with conflict then we need to recognise that conflict is a normal and inevitable part of daily life. Furthermore, conflict can be positive. Through conflict we can learn more about ourselves and others, build better relationships, learn new and better ways of sorting out problems. People can respond to conflicts in helpful or harmful ways and whilst we cannot eliminate conflicts we can learn to resolve them better.

The second fact is that conflict is not a contest. If we assume that the outcome of a conflict will be for one person to "win" and one person to "lose" – or at best for both people to give something up in order to reach a grudging compromise – then, whatever the outcome, one party will feel dissatisfied. Conflict should be viewed as a problem to be solved, so that all people get what they need. The key idea which underpins all creative conflict work is looking for a "win-win" solution.

Thirdly, an essential feature of mediation and conflict resolution is to distinguish between what people want and why they want it. In conflict situations, people often express their wishes (their position) rather than their needs or interests, although it is their unmet needs which underlie the conflict. For example, in the playground, two children are fighting over an apple. The peer helper asks them "What do you want?" They simultaneously reply, "I want the apple." The fellow student then asks each in turn, "What do you need the apple for?" One child wants something to eat, the other wants the seeds for an environmental project. Both can gain in this situation as long as they clearly express their needs.

The mediation/conflict resolution process

In mediation, a neutral third person is called in to mediate. The mediator helps the children to find a solution but does not prescribe what they should do. She or he assists the individuals to recognise what they need and facilitates communication about this. Conflict resolution involves the same process but does not require a third party.

An environment for mediation

The peer mediator will need to ensure that all people who have been involved in the conflict or dispute are present and that the room is sufficiently large for everyone to sit comfortably. The room should be private, with no interruptions. Seating arrangements should reflect the neutrality of the mediator.

Introductions

At the outset, the mediator should remind participants about the purpose of the mediation session and the steps that will be taken within mediation, and repeat some ground-rules about the mediation process. These are that:

- mediation is voluntary
- the mediator remains neutral at all times
- whatever occurs within mediation should remain private and confidential
- the mediation session will last an agreed time
- all parties involved should listen to what is said without interrupting.

Defining the problem

Each participant is given an agreed amount of time to describe their view of the problem situation, without interruptions. Feelings and concerns are heard as well as facts. The mediator clarifies the needs and interests of each party. At the end of each account the mediator summarises what has been said to check for accuracy and to allow both parties to hear and reflect upon this.

Identifying key issues

All issues arising from the accounts are listed on paper. They are divided into non-conflict issues and conflict-related issues.

Visualising an ideal solution

Both parties state ideally what they would like to see happening in the future to improve the situation.

Brainstorm possible options

Both parties are encouraged to suggest solutions to any of the conflict issues identified earlier. These are written down.

Mutual evaluation of potential outcomes of options

Until now, most communication has been directed at the mediator. Now the conversation will become more three-way. The mediator asks each party to think about the outcomes of each solution were it to be implemented, not only for themselves but for each other and for other people.

Negotiation of a plan of action and agreement

The mediator asks the participants, "Which of these solutions will most likely meet the needs of both of you?" One or two solutions are identified. These are clarified to ensure that each party knows who will do what by when and then agreed. A written agreement of future actions is made and signed by all present. Both parties shake hands.

Follow up

A date is made to meet again in the future to evaluate the outcomes of the mediation.

Practising through role play

As with training for peer counselling, the most valuable training experiences will come through role play and continue through discussion in supervision sessions.

Summary

In this chapter we have considered a wide range of training activities for peer support. All types of peer support are based upon good listening skills, respect for self and others, empathy and genuineness. The training programme you design for your school will reflect the type of service you wish to provide. Opportunities for training should continue through on-going supervision.

Part II

Peer Counselling and Support in Action

CHAPTER 5

Children of the Storm: Peer Partnership

Athy Demetriades[1]

In a world full of ever-increasing demands, pressures, insecurities and fears, students have to cope with many issues such as drugs, violence, abuse, divorce, single parent families, lack of money, unemployment.

Schools face tremendous problems. Students tune in and out of school, often wanting to be with their friends. Schools are also changing as the student population becomes more diverse. Belonging to the right social group can mean the difference between "dropping out" and academic achievement. Academically some students find school too difficult and almost impossible to catch up while they have fallen behind. Others find school not challenging enough. Violence and bullying make some children afraid to come to school at all. In the middle of all these conflicts, teachers are trying to teach the future members of our society.

Students helping students is not a new concept in education but how far one school has taken it is perhaps the most important issue. Since 1989 a small number of staff have worked side by side in a rolling programme, unaware of the long-term educational implications, aims or objectives. I am now able to see the achievements of past and present students at Hampstead School and beyond into their futures.

Hampstead School is a typical inner London comprehensive school in the London Borough of Camden, North-West London. It draws on a large catchment area and attracts pupils with a very wide range of abilities and social backgrounds. Over 60 per cent of the student body are bilingual with 87 languages or dialects represented: a true international community. The school prides itself on its equal opportunities policies and has always attempted to celebrate and meet the needs of its international intake.

---

[1]My thanks to Courtney Hawes, an American MA intern from Connecticut University, who after six weeks of observation was able to articulate the process she witnessed and write an inquiry report which has enabled me to compile this chapter; Tamsyn Imison and all the students at Hampstead School; Shirley Pickford; Jenny Carpenter; Children of the Storm; and to the peer partners from whom I have learned and gained so much.

Peer partnership evolved out of a crisis which Hampstead School was faced with in 1989. The turmoil and strife in the world had led children to flee from their countries, many of them unaccompanied minors. Hampstead School was not prepared or trained to deal adequately with the additional special needs these children brought with them: children who had been uprooted from their homes, who had experienced emotional and physical trauma and loss in war-torn, famine-blighted parts of the globe.

In 1989 Hampstead had 29 such children. They came from almost every war-torn country in the world. The numbers have steadily increased over the years; they now total 10 per cent of the school roll. These children have in their lives witnessed perhaps the death of their parents and loved ones. Many of our refugee students have suffered beatings and torture or watched their brothers and sisters killed. All have witnessed the destruction of their homelands. The sixth form at Hampstead School discovered that these children attempt – often with astounding dignity and human spirit – to survive and grow despite the unbearable memories they carry deep within.

The project known as "Children of the Storm" began in 1989. At that time there was no statutory funding available from the government. We had many bilingual students and not nearly enough resources or specialist teaching staff. One particular incident alerted us to the fact that there were actually refugees in the school. Aisha, aged 13 years, arrived from Mogadishu, Somalia. She could understand no English. Hampstead at that time had no formal induction policy. Aisha was introduced to her classmates. Non-verbal communication was all they could offer.

A week later the class introduced her to a game of nudge. From a teacher's point of view it was a great game. It involved all the children and verbal communication was not necessary. A game that began with such promising screams of delight ended abruptly when Aisha had a panic attack which led to her having a heart attack. The class never really recovered from this incident. They never got over the fear they felt when trying to communicate with Aisha. As young adolescents they felt frightened to get close or to reach out to her. However they were extremely watchful; every time Aisha was away or did not arrive at the next lesson, the class had organised themselves in pairs to search for her. On one occasion they found her wandering in the middle of the road outside school with lines of traffic whizzing past her. When she collapsed they were there to stop the traffic and get help. Only afterwards did we learn that the last time Aisha had been nudged was with the butt of a gun before her mother was raped, her father imprisoned and her brother shot and killed.

It was as a direct response to this incident that a group of staff and Aisha's classmates began working together to develop a network of support for refugees, who now account for one in ten of the student body. Our aim was to channel the resources already there in the school; that is, the ability of 1,250 teenagers to make friends and give our refugee students equal access to the curriculum and to the English language.

A joint decision was made by the staff and sixth form on a practical way to help. A four-week training programme gave our student helpers basic skills, covering areas such as second-language acquisition. A number of our refugee students have expressed the pain of feeling isolated in a class full of people – particularly with the language barrier that they all experience in the first few months. The alienation, pain, great sadness and guilt that all these children feel has been the primary inspiration behind our work – the motivation for wanting to touch their lives and show them that someone does care. We cannot of course take away the pain of war or the loss and separation that they feel, but we can be there to lend that helping hand to a fellow human being. Our training programme also covered areas such as understanding the nature of trauma and loss, the past experiences of our refugee children and how to deal with these experiences.

We are extremely fortunate also to have built up a support network which supports the peer partner in his or her role. Listening to a real-life horror story can be extremely frightening and upsetting; it can drain the very life out of one's soul. The peer partners are given the time and space to confront their feelings, to discuss strategies and to come to terms with the pain. They are never left "holding" the pain.

Students are encouraged to talk within a safe environment. Our refugee students are encouraged to attend counselling sessions which are set up in school and led by the Tavistock Clinic. It is not uncommon to watch a peer partner escort their "friend" to a counselling session and 40 minutes later meet them as they walk back to class. It is not uncommon for a peer partner to recommend that counselling to be set up for someone and then to encourage that child to accept the help. This is in fact one area that our peer partners have excelled in and in which they are far more successful than the adults.

The peer partners take their role very seriously as they are then responsible for passing on and re-training the next sixth form. The sorrow, loss and suffering of such children touched the hearts of the sixth form and led to the establishment of Children of the Storm in March 1994 as a separate registered charity. This status was granted in record time so that the charity could pursue its aims to involve young people in helping refugees.

Peer partnership at Hampstead School is a three-way partnership between staff, sixth form and the student body. In addition to the work the sixth form accomplish with the children and the charity, they are also central to the planning and implementation of aims, taking an equal role alongside the trustees of Children of the Storm. As one of our founder peer partners wrote about her role:

> Our job was basically to teach them English and help with homework but most often to be there to chat, play music and generally make them feel they were part of a school community. The support we gave may have been simple but it achieved its aims of integration and understanding.

After the initial four-week training programme the peer partners set up an after-school homework–social club where refugee students could come together and get help with their studies from other students. Very quickly the popularity of the club, now named the "Cocoa Club", grew from strength to strength. Some 80 students are now attending.

Membership has been opened to include anyone who wants to participate. Indeed, the principle of peer partnership extends to fostering friendships between refugee and non-refugee students at all levels in the school. Extra activities include sports and board games with educational impact. There is mixed football for the energetic, Connect Four and chess for compulsive strategists, art workshops led by local artists for the creative and imaginative, and drama workshops for the expressive. So when homework has been done there are opportunities for fun.

Our membership also includes volunteers from the wider community. We have a group of student missionary workers, journalists, fiction writers, university and college students, TV producers and a wonderful mixture of other volunteers. Our own students in the sixth form have discovered a wealth of resources for course work and projects through the experiences and expertise they have gained whilst training others and conducting TV and press interviews. They have also gained valuable experience through putting together the official launch of Children of the Storm, writing to potential patrons, approaching industries for sponsorship and contacting other trusts and charities for project funding. Their success to date is impressive. A concert in March 1993 raised over £6,500. This money has been used to house children, to pay for their bus fares and to pay for school lunches until the paperwork has been cleared. Dame Judi Dench, Geraldine James, Griff Rhys Jones and Lindsay Duncan are our patrons, whilst other trusts and foundations are helping our sixth formers by indicating where and how to bid for additional funding.

In addition to the numerous tasks already outlined, the peer partners are involved in giving advice, brainstorming ideas, helping to deliver and write speeches. Together we decide on a focus for a presentation. With each passing year I am increasingly aware of the inspiring strength that is gained from working alongside them.

One thing that has become very clear over the years is that the skills we have acquired by working with war-traumatised children have influenced the way in which we deal with all our students. Our programme of equality works both ways. It has also greatly lifted the status of the peer partners within the school. They are not just older but far more respected.

As the peer partners work alongside us and the students, they are exposed to extreme examples of mental anguish and trauma. Any one of hundreds of everyday occurrences can break the fragile control of a refugee child.

- A news broadcast
- A school letter sent home addressed to their parents
- A phone call
- Phone lines not operational
- A nudge or a push in a dinner queue
- The mention of a certain month in the year
- Aggression at the mention of "your mum", a very common form of cussing
- A low flying aircraft, or a sudden noise (children have hidden under tables in terror and fear)
- Not being able to recall what a village or loved ones look like
- An adult's signature required for medicals, inoculations or an anaesthetic; this leaves a child wondering who and where to turn to
- The problems of handling money with no guidance – how do you manage on so little? Do you save for a deposit on a flat? Do you eat sensibly, buy books/warm clothes/a jacket/a much-needed desk? Do you just blow it and try and drown your pain?
- The constant thoughts and hopes that a mother, father, brother, sister still lives – grieving cannot begin if just a little hope of their survival remains, no matter how slim
- The heavy burden of guilt they carry with them every minute of every day.

The pain of a child who has suffered mental trauma leaves very little space to concentrate and perform in a class. The subject matter of lessons can also be painful. Pupils in a history lesson were asked to write an account of a conflict. One child's response was: "Everything and everyone is dead."

In another lesson, a discussion on the slave trade resulted in Affrah running out in extreme distress, unable to continue her work. On her long and painful journey to London, the boat Affrah was travelling on broke down. For eight days she watched young men, women and children being thrown overboard, so the boat would not sink. Affrah wants to overcome her fear of water and always chooses a swimming activity for PE but never quite manages to enter the pool.

Other children suffer the frustration of knowing the answers in maths and science lessons, but not being able to communicate them in English, and being put in the low ability groups. These are just a few examples of what these children go through each day and what our peer partners would have to deal with.

Academic success is like a tightrope act. The slightest imbalance can mean disaster. But when our children walk across the playground, they do not walk alone. Many hellos and much laughter can be heard and hugs can be seen. Support with class work and homework means that for just a few hours each day they can be children. When holidays arrive and the school gates are locked these children become isolated and withdrawn ... carrying the unbearable experience of a person years older than 13 or 14.

In the words of Zadie, one of the founder peer partners to become involved in working with refugee children at Hampstead School:

> A lot has been said about the political and legal side of the plight of refugees. But the problem is one on our doorstep. For now we can try to imagine what it's like to be a 15-year-old Somali in an alien classroom. After we have imagined it, we must do something, for the worst crime is apathy. They may not be British citizens, but they are human beings and they are a British responsibility. When the Third World is on your doorstep, it's hard to shut the door in its face.

We have found that the role of the students can and does play a significant part in the well-being of any school community. At Hampstead it has raised the status of refugee students and bilingual learners. It has led to a greater understanding, greater integration and (we hope) a truer equality. The value of friendship is immeasurable and can be a vital lifeline in the midst of today's pressures. There is a unique strength in the support which teenagers are able to give one another: a support which many adults have difficulty in offering and receiving. The greatest tragedy would be that schools fail to do what they can to value all these young people, their special talents, personal inspiration, intelligence, creativity, to instill in them their own worth and potential.

It may be that a sixth-form student joins the peer partnership programme and Children of the Storm out of pity, but that pity then grows to respect for and finally gratitude to the refugee student. As one of our present sixth-formers writes, "You tell me your story, you tell me your plight. As a friend and companion for you I will fight." By utilising older or more knowledgeable students as tutors for individuals or small groups, we as teachers create an interactive learning environment and help to promote and develop communication skills.

The effectiveness and beauty of the peer partnership programme at Hampstead School is that both the tutor and the tutee benefit from the experience. Having students working together enhances the social climate of the school by nurturing responsible attitudes in the students towards one another. The students can then model appropriate behaviour, developing leadership skills at the same time. Learning, friendship and social growth are also among the positive outcomes. Children learn positive attitudes, values and skills through peer partnership. They learn to share, help, comfort and empathise. Peer relationships have a strong influence on achievement. From the student perspective on the influence and benefits of being a peer partner, they almost all agree that they have gained insight and understanding about people and cultures which have grown with their empathy for refugee students.

> "A broader perspective of people's problems."
> "It has made me aware of the world at large and made me thankful for my own position."
> "I have learned that people are the same the world over."

Students also discuss how teaching other students improves their subject knowledge. It would also be true to say that all peer partners working on our project seem to say less about the impact they have had on other students than about how their participation has affected their own lives. Shy, unassuming students have gained in confidence and motivation and their sense of responsibility has increased. For Hampstead School, these and the academic benefits are only part of the goals. Our work has demonstrated the benefits of developing peer partnerships for both the student involved and the school community as a whole.

The term "peer partnership" evolved over a four-week period of brainstorming. We as a team felt it was important to put our role into context. In doing so we have gained a better understanding. The term "peer partnership" gives equal weighting to the peer and the partner.

Both give and both receive, with valuable lessons learnt. Our success is measured when the peer becomes the partner. As schools try to get students involved in positive programmes and improve the school community it is acceptable to say that peer partnership successfully fulfils both objectives.

Schools are committed to helping students but we often overlook the invaluable resource that already exists. Students can and should be trained to help their peers in a variety of ways. This will undoubtedly develop a sense of community and cooperation and ultimately create a place that is safe and nurturing in which children can learn. Peer partnership is for all students, and each should be given the opportunity to develop the potential he or she possesses. If children are to mature into successful adults then actively developing a peer partnership programme is more than a positive school programme: it becomes an essential survival tool for society. Schools must encourage student cooperation and peer partnership so that the healthy development of children and ultimately society may be fostered.

The role of final case study, and indeed tribute, goes to a girl aged 11 years from former Yugoslavia. It is a vivid account of an incident which took place on 14 February 1995: Valentine's Day. The peer partners were engaged in painting love hearts and cards with a number of children. It was a very light-hearted afternoon and the atmosphere was engaging. A great mess had been created, there was lots of laughter and a tape playing in the background. The peer partners had made sure that each child had received a card or drawing. Without warning and, as usual, totally unexpectedly, Ella began her Valentine's card. At first she only wanted to use the black and brown paints. Her partner/friend did not question her choice, merely passed her the colours that she wanted. However, a quick nod alerted another sixth former to come and tell me. At this stage none of us could have predicted the final outcome, nor did we wish to interfere. They both knew that we were there and on hand if we were needed.

Ella covered her large piece of art paper with strong and angry brush strokes, eventually leaving no white showing. She layered the paint thickly and added a few other colours, breaking up the background with streaks of dark blue and then some lighter patches of green, red and yellow. This done, she said, "This is a picture of my mind." Her friend took a deep breath and said that it looked like a mess. "That's how I feel." At this stage she asked her friend to leave her alone so that she could finish her Valentine's card. Ella wanted it to be a surprise. She also wanted it to go up on the ceiling in my office.

That evening the sixth-form team gathered in my small office, something which has become standard after each session of the Cocoa Club. This brief period of time provides one of the most important elements of the peer partnership as it becomes a time for shared experiences and, in this example, the sharing of a tremendously emotional burden, whilst at the same time leaving each sixth former with their own unique experience from the event. Ella had finished her Valentine's card and breezed excitedly into the office where we were gathered, proudly showing us her card. She had completed the card by painting a large red heart over the black and brown background. Inside the red heart she had made smaller hearts, again using the darker colours. Ella then gave each of us a smaller heart, saying she wanted us all to have a piece of her broken heart. The painting of her mind and the rest of her broken heart she put up above my desk. Having transferred her grief she cheerfully left to go home.

It was only this ability and group understanding that enabled the sixth form to come to terms with what they had just witnessed, but through peer partnership they gained a great deal, both in understanding and in the ability to cope with such an experience. Ella had witnessed her father, who had suffered a nervous breakdown, shoot her mother whilst they were taking a bath together.

CHAPTER 6

Creating a Circle of Friends: A Case Study

Gill Taylor

This case study describes the creation of a Circle of Friends for a child whose behaviour was extremely difficult to manage in school.

The rationale behind using this approach is that children with difficult and distressing behaviour frequently become isolated from their peer group and have difficulty in forming friendships. A cycle then develops where feeling excluded and set apart from others leads to behaving in more antisocial ways which then maintain this sense of exclusion from others. Developing a Circle of Friends for a child who may be in this cycle is intended to break this pattern and help the child feel and behave in different ways. It is hoped that the child can achieve a new sense of belonging and acceptance and that this will improve the child's self-image and behaviour. Inherent in this approach is a systemic view of a problem situation where the context the child is in is viewed as maintaining and contributing to the problem (Dowling and Osbourne, 1985). The power of the peer group in affecting a child's behaviour is acknowledged and the aim is to mobilise this force to encourage the child to behave in more socially acceptable ways within the school.

This approach is derived from work in parts of Canada and North America where it is used to support the inclusion of children with disabilities in mainstream schools as well as supporting adults with disabilities within the community (Pearpoint *et al.*, 1992, Perske, 1988). It is a relatively new approach to working with children with emotional and behavioural difficulties in UK schools. Two colleagues and I began using this method in mainstream schools during 1994 with children across the age range, all with extremely challenging behaviour, and we were enthused by the process we were part of and the impact it had on difficult situations (Newton *et al.*, in press).

This approach is a practical one with minimal resource implications. It necessitates involving children who are already in the child's class or tutor group and a key member of staff committing time each week (up to an hour's duration) to meeting with a group of children.

The key aims of this approach are as follows:

1 to create a support network for the child from the immediate peer group
2 to reduce the child's challenging behaviour
3 to enable the child to deal successfully with problems as they arise
4 to increase the child's understanding of their own behaviour and give them more choices
5 to help the child make friends.

This last aim is so easy to write yet so hard for adults to achieve. Here is an approach that can contribute a great deal to this.

Daniel was a Year 6 pupil in a junior school in an inner city area. He had been permanently excluded from his previous school and during his first term at his new school was behaving in a way that others found difficult. This challenging behaviour included physical aggression towards other children in the classroom and in the playground, frequently calling out during class sessions and refusing to cooperate with his class teacher's requests to work.

Daniel's class teacher adopted a positive and firm approach with him and aimed to use rewards to motivate and support him. However, little change occurred during Daniel's first term at school and I was asked to become involved as the school's educational psychologist. By this stage, Daniel's teacher was feeling very frustrated by the seeming lack of change in Daniel's behaviour and his classmates were voicing irritation and dislike towards Daniel.

Deciding to create a Circle of Friends for Daniel

Daniel's behaviour was seen as being extremely disruptive by his class teacher and the headteacher, and he was at risk of being excluded from this school. The usual approaches adopted by the school staff did not seem to be reducing his difficult behaviour.

It was clear that Daniel's behaviour was alienating him from the other children and that he was finding it difficult to make friends. Some children appeared to find his behaviour entertaining but remained distant from him, others seemed frightened by him and there were those that seemed weary of him and the disruption he caused. The class teacher and the headteacher agreed that it would be good to support Daniel in making friends and that this might help him to settle down and adapt better to school life.

I described the Circle of Friends process and the headteacher supported the adoption of this. I explained that it would be the class teacher who would play the key role in supporting and maintaining the Circle and that this would necessitate a weekly meeting of up to an hour's duration with the Circle. The class teacher was keen to engage with this process and a commitment was given that time would be allocated for this weekly meeting.

The headteacher spoke to Daniel's carers and explained the Circle of Friends approach and they agreed to this approach being taken and to support it. I then met with Daniel and talked the situation through with him. I outlined the Circle of Friends approach and asked him if he would be willing for us to do this. Although a little nervous, he seemed enthusiastic about this approach and even asked me to explain to the class that he was having a hard time at home and that this was upsetting him.

Thus the context was in place for creating a Circle of Friends for Daniel.

Note that the following are prerequisites for the Circle of Friends approach:

1 A key member of staff is committed to using the approach and is able to give sufficient time to supporting the Circle of Friends;
2 The child's parent/carer supports this approach being taken;
3 The child accepts this approach being taken.

Initial meeting with the class

I led this initial meeting with the class, which occurred without Daniel being present. He knew what was happening and I agreed with him beforehand to discuss with him the things the class had talked about. The class teacher was present throughout the discussion.

Having been introduced to the class I highlighted the special nature of the discussion. I acknowledged that it was unusual to talk about someone behind their back as we were now doing, but that Daniel had agreed to it and that it was because we wanted to help him be happier at school. We talked about the notion of confidentiality and keeping our discussion within the class. I also stressed how much they were all needed to help in this situation, and that the adults involved were genuinely asking them for that.

I gave two ground rules. Firstly, that we listened to each other and let one person speak at a time. Secondly, that we respected each other's thoughts and feelings and didn't ridicule or criticise them, even if they seemed odd to us.

The class then voiced good things about Daniel and things that they saw as difficult for him and others and I recorded these on a flip chart. The class was eager to contribute to this discussion and able to provide a balanced view of Daniel's behaviour.

Good things about Daniel

- Cheerful
- Says sorry
- Funny
- Helpful
- Plays well
- Honest
- Cleans tables when asked
- Lends things
- Helps people.

Difficult things about Daniel

- Goes where he is not meant to be
- Doesn't listen
- Messy at dinner
- Answers back
- Cheeky
- Impatient
- Calls out
- Ignores the teacher
- Hits and pokes
- Swears at people.

The discussion was then steered towards thinking about life with few or no friends, in order to encourage the children's empathy with Daniel. The children readily contributed to this discussion.

How I would feel if I had few or no friends

- Lonely

- Sad
- Miserable
- Unwanted
- Unhappy
- Angry
- Not special
- Like I had no control
- Bored
- Cut off
- Horrible.

How I would behave

- Be bad
- Fight
- Not do work
- Throw things at people
- Ignore people
- Try to be funny
- Be nasty
- Call people names
- Threaten people
- Run away and hide
- Cry.

The children showed insight into the feelings and behaviour of a person in this situation and generated lots of ideas.

Some of the children then started to make links between this discussion and our previous reflections of Daniel's behaviour. "Daniel tries to be funny but it goes wrong," said one child. "He stops people being nice to him," said another, which led to a discussion of how strange it is that when we want to make friends we sometimes do the very things that upset people and stop us getting what we want. "I don't think Daniel feels wanted here," said one child and others agreed.

It was clear by this stage that many of the children had made the connection that Daniel feeling he had few friends might be contributing significantly to his difficult behaviour. I was touched by the children's obvious concern for Daniel by this stage of the discussion.

The children were then asked to generate ideas for helping Daniel.

- Don't shout at him
- Tell him in a soft way if he is doing something wrong
- Help him with his work

- Ask him to play with us, e.g. football
- Tell Miss if he has problems
- Speak to others who call him names
- Say to Daniel if he gets wound up, "Leave it, it's not worth it"
- Don't crowd him and stare at him if he's in a difficult situation
- Walk home with him
- Ask him to play
- Sit with him at dinner time
- Ask him to help you
- Spend time with him.

This was now the time to ask the children for volunteers to become a Circle of Friends for Daniel. Almost every child in the class volunteered. I selected six children as much at random as possible but purposefully included a child who had begun the discussion on the fringes with his back half turned to me but had become more and more engaged with the process throughout. I talked about this with the class teacher afterwards and discovered that Mark was a child that Daniel had particular problems with and that Mark was also disruptive in the class. We agreed his membership of the Circle would be interesting!

It was important to stress to the other children in the class who weren't in the Circle that they could still help a great deal with Daniel and follow up some of the ideas we had talked about.

The following points should be noted:

1 It is important for an outsider to the class to take the initial meeting to encourage a new perspective on the situation and change the dynamic, although the key member of staff needs to be present. This initial facilitator could be a support teacher, an educational psychologist or possibly someone else within the school, such as the Special Needs Coordinator or year manager.

2 It is always encouraging to see how readily the children can suggest good things about the focus child even when disruption has reached an extreme level.

3 An additional way of helping develop the children's empathy for a person with few or no friends can be to use a visual representation of friendship circles. This is described in Newton *et al.*, in press.

4 The Circle of Friends can be selected in a variety of ways such as by the facilitator, by the key member of staff using his or her knowledge of the children, or truly at random, for instance by drawing out names from a hat. There are pros and cons to each method and this is

something that needs to be discussed and agreed before the class discussion begins.

5 An optimum number for a Circle of Friends is between six and eight children.

Initial Circle meeting

We had the first Circle meeting immediately after the class discussion. Both the class teacher and myself were present with Daniel and the six other children.

I led the first Circle gathering and began by reminding the Circle of the two ground rules I had previously given, and explained them to Daniel. The Circle also agreed to keep discussions within these meetings confidential.

We then talked with Daniel about the class discussion, particularly focussing on how keen the class were to help him feel happier and more settled in school. Daniel was clearly very happy to hear that so many people wanted to be in his Circle.

Each child in the Circle then said why they wanted to be in Daniel's group of friends and we agreed that the key aims were to stop Daniel getting into trouble as much and for him to get on better with the other children and adults in the school. We discussed what the Circle would be named and the children agreed on "The Helping Group".

We then went through all the ideas the class had generated for helping Daniel and talked these through in more detail. Particular approaches were discussed and the children practised making specific statements in certain situations.

Circle of Friends agreed approaches

- One or two of them sit with him at dinner
- One of them sit next to him in class
- Ask him to play with them at playtime
- Ask him if he needs help with his work
- If he starts getting into trouble say, "Leave it, it's not worth it", "Calm down, it's all right".
- Remind him of the good things about him
- Ask why
- Try and get his attention on to something else.

We talked about getting the balance right between helping Daniel and not "crowding" him. I also emphasised that the children had agreed to help Daniel but they weren't responsible for him and his work and behaviour – that was still the adults' responsibility.

On-going Circle meetings

These were weekly and facilitated by the class teacher. They lasted between 30 and 40 minutes. The structure of these meetings was:

1. review the good things about the past week, including all of Daniel's and the Circle's achievements
2. discuss the difficulties that have arisen during the week, including when and where they happened and possible reasons for them
3. generate ideas for dealing with the difficulties.

The teacher's role here is to help the children stay focussed during these discussions, encourage all to contribute and guide the problem-solving approach.

Daniel's teacher kept notes of the weekly Circle meetings and below is an example of one of them. (This meeting was four weeks after the initial meeting.)

Good things

- Better at eating at lunchtime, less messy
- Getting on with work better
- Getting better at spelling
- Not missing playtimes now
- We are his friends now.

Difficulties

- Daniel said the Helping Group were asking if they could help him with his work a bit too often.
- Children in other classes were "calling" Daniel.
- Daniel and Mark were swearing at each other during football at playtime.

Agreed approaches

- Daniel would now ask for help if he needed it with his work.
- Daniel would speak to the teacher if he needed to about other children, or just think and say, "Leave it, it's not worth it."

- Daniel and Mark agreed to try to be friendly, even when on different football teams. They also agreed to try to sometimes be on the same team.

These are brief notes of a Circle meeting and do not include the rich, insightful dialogue that often occurred, some of which their teacher recorded and examples of which are included later.

As the outside facilitator, I agreed to stay in touch with their class teacher by phone discussion and to attend a Circle meeting five weeks after the initial meeting.

Negotiating an ending to the Circle

After seven weeks of weekly meetings the Helping Group decided that bi-weekly meetings would now be sufficient. This was because of the significant improvement in Daniel's behaviour; and because the class were now in their final term of junior school, they knew an ending was imminent. It was agreed by the children and their teacher that moving to a bi-weekly meeting would help this ending happen gradually. As Tom said, "Daniel doesn't need a Circle any more because now we're his friends."

In the penultimate week of the summer term, I attended the final meeting of the Circle and each child had the opportunity to reflect on being involved. All were positive and each said they would be part of a Circle again if the opportunity ever arose. Daniel thanked each member of his Helping Group.

The following points should be noted:

1 It is important to emphasise that the children are not responsible for the focus child. Working with a Circle of older children, I have seen some become upset, thinking that their friend getting into trouble is their failure. The children need reminding that they are helping but that the adults are still responsible.
2 The focus child can use being a member of the Circle as a reward or threat to other children. Daniel initially did this; it was very important that his Helping Group talked about this and it was seen that the group was democratic and voluntary, not "owned" by Daniel.
3 The content of Circle meetings can vary a great deal in terms of their emotional content. It is important that the adult facilitating the group

maintains boundaries and keeps the discussion feeling safe for all. The group is not a formally therapeutic one, but I have no doubt that these kinds of discussions have the potential to enable children to reflect on and come to terms with difficult feelings and experiences.

4 The Circle provided a good forum for Daniel and Mark to sort out some of their problems with each other, with the help of others.

5 With Daniel's Circle there was a natural ending as the children were leaving the school. With other Circles we have agreed to finish meeting by the end of a particular half-term or term and then to meet a term later just to review things. This gradual way of ending seems to be the most comfortable for the children involved.

Summary of the process of creating a Circle of Friends

1 Establishing prerequisites for the approach.
2 Initial meeting with class without focus child present.
3 Creating a Circle of Friends and having the initial meeting.
4 Ongoing meetings of Circle.
5 Negotiating ending of Circle of Friends.

Outcomes for Daniel

A key outcome was that Daniel was not excluded. He was at risk of this, but this support enabled him to end his junior school career with a lot of successes.

His class teacher identified the following outcomes of the Circle of Friends for Daniel:

- Less frequent shouting out
- More commitment to work and pleasure in completing tasks
- More humour
- No aggressive outbursts
- Developed healthy friendships
- Increased ability to express his thoughts and feelings.

In the final meeting of the Circle, Tom said he felt that Daniel had changed a lot and Daniel agreed, saying he felt calmer inside.

I have since received reports from the Special Needs Coordinator of Daniel's secondary school that he has progressed well academically and socially during Year 7. Any problems that have arisen have been tackled and contained within the school's internal system.

Effects on other members of the Circle

It was evident to the class teacher that all of the children gained from the experience of being part of a Circle of Friends. From the outset, she and I agreed that this was a lively and meaningful approach to personal and social development for the children. Her notes of discussions during Circle meetings indicate this.

The following elements of a PSE (Personal and Social Education) curriculum were all part of the children's experience of being part of a Circle of Friends.

Developing empathy

It was evident during discussions in the Circle meetings that the children were putting themselves into Daniel's shoes and imagining his feelings.

> Tom: Daniel gets done to for being fostered and that's not right because he feels bad then.
> Lauren: He's sad enough about it without getting called about it.
> Daniel: I get upset and I want to beat them up.
> Mark: I know a bit about how Daniel feels because my sister had to have a social worker.

After the closure meeting, Lauren wrote something of her experience of being in Daniel's group:

> Daniel's Friends
>
> When we started being in Daniel's Helping group we felt OK and when we heard of Daniel's Dad we felt sorry for him. Daniel said he locked him in his room. It made Clare feel very sad and it made me feel sad and Clare thought Daniel looked a bit sad too. Me and Clare feel kind of angry with his Dad but it was in the past. We feel happy being Daniel's friends. (Lauren, aged 11)

Developing problem-solving skills

At each Circle meeting the children discuss problems that have arisen and think about ways to address them.

> Tom: When people are getting picked on at play, Daniel tries to help and then he gets into bother.
> Teacher: What ideas have you got for helping with that problem?

Clare: We could just say to Daniel, "Leave it, it's not worth it."
Daniel: But they wind me up when they're calling people.
Mark: You could just tell the teacher.
Lauren: Maybe Daniel could talk to one of us and we could decide whether to talk to the teacher or the other children or just leave it.
Teacher: So you could make a joint decision about what to do?
Daniel: I could talk to Tom when it happens in football.
Lauren: And then to any of us.

This plan of making a joint decision was agreed by all.

Developing listening skills

The two ground rules for Circle meetings encourage the development of listening skills. The children have the opportunity to practise taking turns in listening to each other, commenting on what they have heard and valuing each other's contributions.

Developing the ability to express thoughts and feelings

The Circle's meetings allow the focus child to express in a safe environment their thoughts and feelings regarding their problems and to seek support. The other children see these as being accepted and this encourages them to view their own feelings and thoughts as being valid.

At some points, the other children may introduce their own personal experiences.

David: I've moved house six times since my Gran died and I'm sad about that.
Hinal: I get sad when my Mum and Dad shout at each other.

It is important at these times for the facilitator to keep boundaries whilst acknowledging and appreciating the contribution of each child.

Developing an understanding of the links between feelings and behaviour

This can be a difficult connection for adults to make as well as for children. The Circle of Friends approach provides a rich opportunity for seeing that people's behaviour cannot always be taken at face value. Sometimes the most aggressive people are the most frightened or sad. Sometimes the most unfriendly are the ones most wanting a friend. These insights can give children a delightfully generous view of others, even though they still want their unpleasant behaviour to stop.

Hinal: After play Daniel sometimes runs round the classroom bothering people.
Tom: I think sometimes Daniel tries too hard because he feels nobody wants him.
Hinal: You don't have to run round the room, Daniel, just talk to us.

Developing an increased awareness of people's capacity to change their behaviour

Throughout the lifetime of a Circle, the other children can see how a child whose behaviour was extremely disruptive can change. Frequent comments are made about this.

Lauren: Daniel's much less messy at dinner now, he has really tried hard to change that.
David: Daniel doesn't call out all the time now, he gets on with his work.

This is what Tom wrote after the final Circle meeting:

> From the beginning we felt Daniel had something wrong with him. He made a few friends but he had a few problems. A person called Gill Taylor came to talk about Daniel's problems with the class. We decided to have a group to help Daniel. The group decided to meet every week in the afternoon. It was hard work trying to get Daniel under control. Daniel was getting hard done to about being fostered. We don't think that is fair on Daniel. He had a lot of problems in the classroom, like shouting out, cheeking the teacher and mucking about. We think Daniel has learnt and changed a lot. (Tom, aged 11)

To see that people can change how they behave can give hope and optimism about others' difficult behaviour as well as making us think at times of our own!

Concluding comments

Creating Circles of Friends for children who are experiencing difficulties with school life is a powerful and exciting process. This approach achieved a great deal in Daniel's situation and it has proved to be effective in many other cases (for further descriptions of these see Newton *et al.*, in press).

The transformations that happen within a Circle involve the best of open and honest human contact. A group is created where feelings are accepted and valued and a cooperative approach is taken to solving problems. The climate within the Circle is a non-judgemental, hopeful one and enables a child who has previously been at odds with others to feel more accepted and liked. The emphasis is on the inclusion of the focus child within the school community and reducing experiences of exclusion.

A child's peer group can strongly influence a child and give them a new perspective on a situation. "Leave it, it's not worth it" somehow sounds very different coming from a peer compared with the way it sounds coming from someone who is in authority. Children can be powerful allies to each other and strong advocates.

As described here, all the children involved in the Circle appear to gain from the experience, not just the focus child. It would be good to explore this aspect of Circle life further. Helmstetter *et al.* (1994) investigated the outcomes for peers involved with the inclusion of focus children with moderate and severe disabilities and their results indicate a developed sense of personal responsibility and an ethic of caring and commitment to others. These initial findings are very encouraging.

The members of staff involved frequently say that they have benefitted from the experience; they feel supported and more positive, and as the focus child's behaviour changes, they have less disruption to contend with. I have gained a great deal from witnessing the generosity, frankness and care shown by children towards each other and have been encouraged by seeing significant changes in very difficult situations.

This is an inclusive approach to supporting some of our most troubled children and one which can also be used with a wide variety of people in a range of settings. (For more of this in the UK see Neville, 1995.) Even though it is a simple approach in many ways, it can be a life-changing experience for children and adults alike.

The last word belongs to Mark:

Me and Daniel

At first I did not like Daniel. I got good friends with Daniel. I enjoy being in Daniel's group. I would be in it again. (Mark, aged 10)

CHAPTER 7

Three Years in the Life of a Peer Counselling Service

Anne Sellors

Setting up the service

In September 1991 our school became one of the DFE Sheffield Bullying Project schools. It is a split-site comprehensive of 985 pupils, situated on a large council housing estate in Sheffield. It caters for pupils aged 11–16.

Denise Watson, the head, was highly committed to the project. Throughout the academic year 1991/2 all staff, parents, governors and pupils had considered and developed a school policy document on bullying. A group of pastoral staff had also prepared curriculum-based strategies for awareness raising and discussion work. Sonia Sharp and Helen Cowie, members of the research team, discussed with me an idea for developing a peer counselling service in school.

The intention was to provide a peer counselling service in school specifically for those who were suffering from being bullied. The school already had in place systems for pupils to tell their form tutors, Heads of Year, and staff "on call". They were also encouraged to tell parents or friends if they could. This peer service was for those who found it impossible to do any of the above but who might feel more at ease with a peer. Together they could then explore the "client's" anxieties and discuss ways in which the problem might be alleviated.

To emphasise the importance of the role of the "Bullyline counsellor", pupils were invited to apply formally in writing giving details of their reasons for wanting to be involved as well as describing what they could offer to the role. Candidates were interviewed and took part in two half-day training sessions which introduced the pupils to basic active listening skills and provided them with an opportunity to practise them. The pupils learned how to be good listeners, to refrain from interrupting, to paraphrase, to be comfortable with silence and emotion. They were taught about body language and social distancing. They were also given extra twilight sessions of two hours a time, once the service was up and running, to develop their skills. During the training, great emphasis was placed upon confidentiality. This confidentiality was set within certain parameters. Should a pupil be told that someone was being badly hurt or sexually abused, they were required to refer to the named member of staff. The counsellors were provided with a script (which they all practised) for such occasions as follows:

> I am sorry. I cannot help you with this, you need to tell a member of staff. Shall we go and find someone now?

The counsellors were briefed never to promise secrecy. If the pupil refused to talk with a member of staff, the Bullyline counsellor was still required to seek out the key member of staff to let them know what was going on.

The counsellors represented a good cross-section of the school's population, although there were certain year groups who did not respond. Thirty-eight pupils were accepted out of the 40 who applied. They came from Years 7, 9, 10 and 11. We were fortunate too, to have a good male/female divide. Many of the boys had a certain "street cred" which helped the service to be accepted by the pupils.

Not all the pupils who joined the Bullyline were immediately used as counsellors. Whilst the training sessions and twilight sessions were in progress the trainers noted who was ready to counsel and who still needed more rehearsal. The latter were initially given administrative posts, such as receptionist, filing clerk. This would give these pupils a later chance to develop their counselling skills. It also helped to give the service a receptionist's area where clients could book in to see specific counsellors or to make their next appointment.

The problem of finding a room available from which to run the service was solved when a year tutor allowed us to use his office at lunchtimes. (There were also two other rooms available if there were two or more clients at the same time.) This room was in an outer building which was not in use at lunchtime as it housed the music and drama rooms. It was not in the main building where the great majority of pupils ate and congregated. This prevented upset clients from being seen by hordes of pupils.

In the early days, the service ran for three days a week from 11.40 to 12.30 each lunchtime. On the fourth day we held a group meeting to review the week, problems encountered by the counsellors, and to share good practice. Chief amongst the fears expressed by the counsellors, prior to the launch of the service, was their being confronted by a problem that was too demanding for them to deal with.

Each counsellor has a file containing record sheets. After each appointment they note the gender and age of the pupil they have been listening to as well as brief notes about the nature of their client's problems. Each client is given a personal code number. The recording helps the counsellors to remember who they have seen, but more importantly, it enables me to monitor its usage. These files are kept securely in the Bullyline office. I am always on call to support the counsellors if they need it.

As the time commitment is a major factor in this work, counsellors commit themselves to a term at a time. At the end of each term they can opt out. Other pupils are on standby to deputise in case of illness. (Three girls gave two years' service and then opted out; one took a year off in Year 10 and rejoined in Year 11.)

We decided to launch the line by advertising it through the bully bulletin – a weekly newsletter going out to all forms. Those first weeks of any peer counselling service are the most difficult. The counsellors are all geared up to expecting their first client and nobody appears. I had to discourage the counsellors from wanting to go on to the corridors, grab someone round the neck and say "You *have* got a problem, now tell me about it!"

However, by November there was a steady trickle of customers and there were discussions on how to broadcast our service. As head of drama I was already looking at the issue of bullying – what is a bully – in an improvised performance piece with the Year 11 GCSE drama group. The year team too were performing a scripted play entitled *The Terrible Fate of Humpty Dumpty* which focusses on the worst consequences of bullying.

We therefore harnessed these pieces to target Years 7, Year 8 and Year 9 assemblies using the performances as a focus to discuss bullying. Members of Bullyline would then inform the pupils as to their role and describe what exactly happens when someone comes to use the service.

This effectively was the turning point because the counsellors impressed both pupils and staff with their professional, mature delivery and a trust grew in the service. Whilst we had been thinking that it was important for the counsellors to keep a low profile and remain basically anonymous it was the reverse that proved to be true. Once we realised this, we clearly displayed photographs of the counsellors on the main corridors. Leon, one of the team, designed a dramatic black and white logo which we then used on posters, stationery and dinner pass cards.

Empowering the pupil counsellors

There is strong need for control within the heart of most teachers. I was learning that, whilst I was trying to control the administration of the files, the publicity of the service and other vital tasks, I was often failing to meet the deadlines that we had set ourselves. The counsellors at one meeting pointed this out to me and showed how much more effective they would be at producing rotas/ appointment cards/ liaising with the head and other staff. This was all too true, and with their organisation the service improved immensely and has continued to improve over the years.

In our first year one of our most effective counsellors was Sarah. She was a mature, professional pupil in her fourth year who also had cerebral palsy. A feature of at least one twilight session was a sharing of the times when we had all suffered bullying or indeed had been bullies. The experiences of Sarah really brought home to us the ignorance of so many people in their attitude towards those with a disability. Sarah also suffered this ignorance from many pupils at school.

She volunteered to lead a Year 7 assembly to address this problem. Other counsellors volunteered to help her by role-playing situations that she had encountered. This was a moving, impassioned description of her life and her illness. The Year 7 pupils followed this up with curriculum-based assignments which hopefully helped to change their attitudes towards disability. The assembly also proved to be the catalyst for a young girl to start to talk at last about the death of her parents and the fear of her only remaining guardian (who was also disabled) dying. It became clear that encouraging talk between peers encourages more talk between staff and pupils on all sorts of subjects.

Another concern was to encourage talk between children and their parents. The peer counsellors and drama groups held an evening of performance and discussion with parents through the PTA. This again brought forth disclosures from some parents as to their unhappiness through bullying at school when they were children and when they are at work.

Monitoring the service and facilitating change

Quality control is a very difficult issue in peer counselling. One trusts that the counselling session is well conducted and constructive. I was concerned at the speed with which one counsellor was conducting his sessions. He would announce after five minutes at the most that he "had sorted everything out". After discussing this as a group with the counsellor, we mutually decided that maybe his skills would be better used as our main administrative officer. He has proved to be the lifeblood of the service – keeping the statistics, coordinating meetings, creating new computer programs.

His desire to solve a client's problems immediately was perfectly understandable and was often voiced as the greatest temptation of all the counsellors. We all want immediate resolutions to problems but we have to learn that life isn't like that. Learning to encourage clients to examine their situation and to explore all manner of different resolutions can give them more options to choose from and a greater sense of self-worth. This is another discussion point that returns and returns in the review sessions.

After looking at all their options, clients will frequently choose the option of asking the peer counsellor to mediate on their behalf. This may take the form of verbalising a client's experience, to a form teacher, to a client's friend, to a head of year or to the bully themselves.

Sometimes the client will ask for the peer counsellor to explain how they are feeling to the bully whilst the client is in the room. An atmosphere of complete trust has to have developed between client and counsellor. These sessions have always proved constructive – frequently the bully has no idea of how their behaviour has affected the client. The bully is often deeply upset and apologetic.

In one session a client complained about being pushed and thumped by a boy who was actually a friend of the counsellor. Sean, the counsellor, felt compelled to tell the client that he was actually a friend of the aggressive boy. At the request of the client the counsellor brought the two boys together and the bully disclosed that he was being bullied himself. He wanted to make someone else feel the same way he did. He wanted to feel the power that he lacked when he was being bullied. Sean continued to counsel both boys together and separately until both clients felt happier and their situations were resolved.

Another case study from that first year is the situation of R. She told her counsellor that she was feeling sick but she couldn't say why. Eventually after a number of counselling sessions it emerged that she was feeling sick before a particular lesson where she was having trouble with one of her teachers.

R. was asked by the counsellor to keep a diary of incidents. There were shown in a separate session by the counsellor to the teacher in question. The teacher was deeply surprised and worried by what she saw in the diary. She had no idea that her comments to R. had been seen in such a negative light. The teacher talked to R. in depth until a new and greater understanding had been reached. This supportive reaction by the teacher we found to be indicative of the way in which the staff had learnt to trust the service.

By the end of our first year, it was fascinating to see the development in maturity and experience of the peer counsellors. Several of them had been victims themselves, hence their desire to help others in a similar situation. This has been one of the greatest spin-offs of the whole process, empowering a pupil to become a leading expert in a field of life where they had only ever been a victim. This development was leading them into meeting pupils from other schools from as far afield as London – pupils wishing to set up their own peer counselling projects. Visitors from the DFE, European universities and local radio all helped to give the counsellors a greater sense of their own worth.

Into the second year of the project: emerging problems

Gender issues

We lost several excellent counsellors when they went on to further education in the new academic year. This gave us an uneven distribution of male/female counsellors – we had many more girls than boys. So we advertised rigorously for boys to consider joining the service.

We are a school, like many others, where our boys underachieve and do less well at GCSE level than girls. The "line" felt it important that we should be seen to be a service of equal opportunity. As we were still running assemblies and performances for the new Year 7 intake and reminding Years 7, 8 and 9 of our work, we felt that the visual presence of male counsellors would inspire others to consider joining the service.

In retrospect there was a backlash to this. Because we maybe overemphasised the need for males, and because training sessions were not as many and as long this first term, owing to financial and academic commitments, certain problems arose.

The chief problem was that some of the boys acting as receptionists began to take liberties with the Bullyline reception office. On rainy days they would congregate in the office when it wasn't their duty day, thus causing a threat to the service. If any distraught client were to walk in to make an appointment this would surely scare them off immediately.

They also abused the lunch pass system, using it on days when they were not on duty. This in turn brought anger and frustration from lunchtime supervisors, who had supported the service, often bringing clients to it.

The final straw was when one of the trainee counsellors spilt Coke on the teacher's desk in the office, mopped it up with tissues and then left them on the desk for the teacher to find! We were banned from using his office for two weeks.

Such behaviour can quickly bring a service into disrepute with both pupils and staff. After an emergency session with all the counsellors, three trainee counsellors were deprived of their position – it was unanimously agreed by their peers that they had used the service for their own perks rather than contributing to it.

The behaviour of peer counsellors themselves

Another factor which can sometimes come into play is the behaviour of counsellors in and around school. It would be very damaging if counsellors themselves were perceived as bullies. One counsellor during Year 9 had a spate of losing his temper and getting into very serious fights. After the second fight he came to see me. He was aware that he was failing to control his moods and therefore felt that he should step down until he felt more in control of himself. He has not yet returned to the service.

In this second year we had been given a small amount of money, £100, from the proceeds of the Christmas disco. After discussion the group decided to use it to fund one of the older and most experienced counsellors to go on a course on "fogging", a technique used to help victims of bullying. Nicola then came back and ran training sessions for us all to use this new strategy.

The impact of the media

We were approached by the press and television in this second year to give interviews and be filmed. This was our most painful learning experience – we quickly learnt that a peer counselling service primarily dealing with clients who have been bullied was not really the main focus of newspaper articles. One newspaper journalist came and then wrote an article about the school which paid lip service to the Bullyline but which emphasised and exaggerated examples of bullying in school. All this could do was damage the school image and do little to promote confidence in our press. Ironically they were knocking a school which was openly saying that there is bullying in every school, including ours, and that we are trying to do something about this problem. Far better to question the schools which still stated that they had no bullying in their institution.

Television crews too filmed us, raised hopes amongst staff and pupils alike and then failed even to mention us in their programmes. We learned to say no; we learned to appreciate that no publicity was good publicity; we learnt to question our need for publicity anyway. The counsellors discovered more about the dangers of the press in three months than I had in 40 years. They are now adept at fielding questions. They give very few interviews and then only to responsible, principled reporters.

Building close relationships

Experiences like these have helped to make the counsellors an incredibly close, warm community. When you sit in a small office with another person for an hour, without a client appearing, you discuss so much, you share so much. A major spin-off from the service has been the flowering of friendship, frequently between pupils two or three years apart in age as we try to put younger, less experienced counsellors on at the same time as the older ones. This capacity to form and sustain close relationships with other children is a quality which many of our clients find very hard.

One client came to Stacey very upset and complaining about headaches. He was a new Year 7 pupil who was clearly ill at ease and unhappy. He said that he was having problems with his maths – Stacey saw his maths teacher for him at his request. With this problem solved, he still returned to Stacey for several weeks until he felt safe enough to tell her the real reason for his headaches. His parents had recently split up. He was living with mum but was desperately missing his dad. He did not like to upset his mother further by saying that he wanted to see his dad. Stacey suggested that she pretend to be his mother and he could practise on her how to tell his mother this. After a couple of sessions he became confident enough to tell his mother, who listened and agreed to letting him see his father. With this solved, he has become a highly successful happy pupil within the school.

Aware of this, by the end of year two of the Bullyline some of the counsellors had also set up the "Buddyline" on their own initiative. The "buddies" would befriend a form – take them to different classrooms throughout the day and look out for the more isolated and lonely pupils who could well be targets for bullying. This hopefully then gave those new pupils someone to depend upon in the early weeks of the new term when they most needed it.

Benefits to the counsellors

The qualities of maturity and confidence which initiatives like these have helped to develop have also led to benefits for the peer counsellors themselves. For example, by the end of year two both Sarah and Nicola (Year 11 leavers) were going on to college to take psychology as one of their A levels. Many of the counsellors have now gained enough insight and experience in their work on Bullyline to want to take this experience further into their careers.

Similarly our third year of running the service has turned several of the counsellors into highly adept "after-dinner speakers". We have been invited to contribute at two major national conferences, one on bullying held in Sheffield and one on peer counselling held in London. The confidence and ease with which the pupils address the audience of 50 to 80 professional adults reflects the other benefits to be gained from running a service.

We earn money from these conferences which can aid training and travel. Some of our payment from the London conference paid towards a wonderful extra day in London where we saw the sights and stayed in a youth hostel in Hampstead. Travel broadens horizons – in the hostel the counsellors stayed up into the early hours talking to fellow students from all over the world.

Other spin-offs have been making a training video for Helen Cowie and Sonia Sharp. How fortunate have we been to have worked for three years with such inspirational people as Helen, Sonia, Gerard Walsh, Barbara Lawton and Jim Lewis. Their knowledge and experience has in turn informed and enriched our service.

Few school-based initiatives can demand so much commitment from the pupils. They had to be prepared to train not only in school time but at lunchtimes and after school. Frequently they have trained on Saturdays too, looking specifically at training through video analysis of their counselling skills. Their time is demanded for at least two lunchtimes every week, as well as assembly rehearsals (at least two hours after school), producing training videos on Saturdays, spending endless time preparing for conferences. With experience, of course, this does grow easier because there is more material and experience to draw on. This same commitment is demanded from the staff who are prepared to help run it.

Does peer counselling tackle the problem of bullying?

In terms of the school community an obvious question to ask is "Yes, but is it working? Is it helping to stop bullying?"

The figures for pupils saying that they are being bullied are not dropping but then for the last three years staff, Bullyline and assemblies have all been preaching the message that "Telling is OK". This will inevitably encourage more reported incidents. The perception that "school is a place where something is done about bullying" was held by 91 per cent of our Year 7 pupils in a survey conducted last year. Many parents specifically opt for their pupils to come to us because we take a positive stance against bullying. Four major challenges face us at present:

- The counsellors are preparing a pilot scheme to include parents more in the process of helping a client – their child – if the client wishes it.
- There is a shared concern that we are not doing enough at present to encourage those perceived as bullies to come along to talk to and use the service. Our funds this year will be targeted at researching this area and running some trial projects.
- We need to develop and tighten up on our record keeping and on our clients' assessment feedback sheets.
- We would like to develop an assertiveness package for the least assertive clients. We will have to spend time raising the necessary funding to achieve this goal.

Running and developing a service creates a vehicle which encourages young people to take on responsibility, to become more aware of the hopes and fears of their peers. It encourages young people to become experts in an area of life that many adults have problems with. It develops their communication skills, oracy, confidence, self-reliance and problem-solving skills, and opens up a window of opportunity for their future. Half an hour in the company of our counsellors is better than winning a million pounds on the lottery!

CHAPTER 8

Combatting Bullying in School: The Role of Peer Helpers

Netta Cartwright

I am a teacher and school counsellor in a large state comprehensive mixed-sex secondary school in Stafford for 11- to 18-year-old students. Over the last five years I have been leading the development of a whole-school anti-bullying policy. It began as an idea from the students and has continued to be implemented by them with me as their ally.

Five years ago a group of students from the school council asked me, as the school counsellor, what I thought could be done to stop bullying in school. Some of them represented the school in the Crime Concern Trust, a charity financed by insurance companies and supported by the police and social services. I suggested they get the police and this charity to provide financial support and publicity for a workshop in our school. This was done and I organised a whole-school day workshop led by me and Michele Elliott from Kidscape, a national organisation campaigning against bullying in schools.

Michele led the morning and I led the afternoon. The morning session was in the big school hall and was attended by student and teacher representatives from the other schools in Stafford and student representatives from each tutor group in my school. Michele talked about anti-bullying strategies, including bully courts, used in other schools and then had the students working in groups to discuss strategies they could use in their own schools to stop bullying.

In the afternoon session I arranged for the representatives to go back to their schools and tutor groups and replicate the activities done in the morning. Each student became a leader with older Year 12 and 13 students (17- to 18-year-olds) as allies, previously briefed by me. Teachers were to provide non-participating support and had also been briefed by me. The afternoon was structured to allow for discussions in groups of twos and threes leading to a list of ideas from each tutor group and a decision on whether they wanted a school policy, an anti-bullying contract to be signed by all and/or bully courts run by students.

This all took place and the written decisions and ideas were collated by the school's anti-bullying working party (all students) and reported back to the whole school. The consensus was to have a whole-school anti-bullying policy which would include a contract signed by all students and a peer counselling service run by students for bullies and survivors of bullying. They did not want bully courts.

The whole-school anti-bullying policy

This is the anti-bullying policy which has evolved at Walton High School:

- The school has a definition of bullying and all students sign a contract of behaviour
- The guidelines for student behaviour are posted on boards throughout the school
- There is a clear procedure to follow should bullying occur and everyone knows what it is
- A student helper scheme enables volunteers from Years 11-13 to learn basic counselling and listening skills so they can offer counselling to all years and be attached to Year 7 and Year 8 tutor groups
- There is a sanctions and support system for bullies, including counselling as above
- There is a rewards system for non-aggressive behaviour
- The school's physical environment and general organisation is not conducive to bullying behaviour
- There is full involvement of teaching and non-teaching staff, governors, parents and students in discussion and implementation of the anti-bullying policy
- The curriculum includes:

1 A PSE programme for students to discuss the policy, support, monitor and update it;
2 Assemblies, drama productions and other means of raising awareness on the subject.

The workshop had an influence and other schools in Stafford are working on developing anti-bullying strategies which involve students as tutor group leaders and peer helpers. A teacher in a nearby school joined forces with me and we introduced students from our respective schools' working parties to each other. We went with them to three national conferences of the Crime Concern Trust where the pupils talked about what they were doing to stop bullying in their schools. In our school the anti-bullying policy's most public action is twofold: the anti-bullying contract and the student helper scheme.

The anti-bullying contract

Four years ago I organised assemblies to discuss the contracts, at which the students voted on the workshop proposals. The outcome is the pupil contract which is signed by all pupils at the school and by their parents.

Box 8.1 A pupil contract

Representing the general will of all pupils at Walton High School after full consultation.
A. I will treat my fellow pupils with respect;
B. I will not humiliate or hurt any other pupil physically or verbally;
C. I will do the best I can to help any pupil who is obviously being upset or hurt by one or more other pupils.

Pupil's signature ....

PARENTS:
I have read the above and will do my utmost to ensure that my son/daughter will abide by this contract.

Parent's signature ....

All students signed it and all new students sign it on joining the school. Their parents also sign it, saying they will support their young person in abiding by it. Year 7 students are introduced to the contract in their first few weeks at school during assemblies, drama productions and discussions in personal and social education lessons led by student helpers.

Peer counselling: the student helper scheme

Four years ago I also began the process of setting up the peer counselling service. I asked for volunteers from Years 11, 12 and 13 (15- to 18-year-olds). About 40 students were very keen to learn. In the first two years I taught four short Re-evaluation Counselling courses with about ten students in each course. Each course consisted of six classes of an hour's length. They took place after school in the school building. The students learned basic listening skills and co-counselling skills. I demonstrated counselling and they co-counselled in the classes and in between.

Box 8.2 The basics of co-counselling

Co-counselling is an agreement between two people to take it in turn to listen to each other. When someone really listens to you it is easier to get rid of bad and confusing feelings which stop you thinking clearly. When you have got them out of your system, you can think of ways to solve any problems you may have.

How to listen properly

Be like this to your friend	*Do not be like this*
caring and interested	soppy or bossy
look at your friend	look around the room
respectful	overbearing or nosy
delighted to see her or him	disapproving or uninterested
thinking	routine or just pretending to listen
encouraging and accepting	judgemental or unsympathetic
confident	hesitant or apologetic
encourage feelings to come out	stop your friend from laughing, crying, being angry, etc
encourage your friend to think of their own solutions to problems	give advice or easy answers

Two years ago I taught sixteen students from Year 12 (17-year-olds), a longer course with an 18-year-old assistant who had already been taught by me previously. The course included a residential weekend and amounted to 24 hours. Last year my headteacher gave me more time on my teaching timetable for teaching counselling so that we could extend the service. Sixty-eight students aged 15-18 have volunteered to do the courses and become student helpers. By the end of the year they were all going into Year 7 and 8 tutor groups on a regular basis. The basics of co-counselling are shown in Box 8.2.

During training, students, working in pairs, are asked to take it in turns to listen for three minutes each way. They are asked questions like:

What makes it difficult for you to listen properly?

In what situation would you like to be a better listener?

How are you a good listener already?

The theory behind the training is that of Re-evaluation Counselling (RC). This theory is based on the assumption that we live in a world and universe that is essentially benign. Human beings, at birth and at heart, are innately intelligent, energetic, clear-thinking, loving, lovable and eager to learn, communicate and cooperate with others. The theory also assumes that we have all been hurt so that our ability to think and function well has been impaired by the stress and distress acquired in the process of growing up in a society structured on inequality, injustice and pressure to compete and conform. RC recognises that everyone has the natural and inherent ability to recover from the effects of the hurts they have experienced. This automatically occurs through a process of emotional release or "discharge" that includes laughing, crying, raging, yawning, shaking, trembling, blushing, sweating and animated talk. The problem is that these processes of discharge are inhibited, or even appear to be extinguished, through a misunderstanding of their meaning. People mistakenly equate the discharge with the hurts instead of recognising it as the healer of the distress. So, as we grow older, we are strongly discouraged or forbidden to discharge in certain ways depending on our gender, class, etc. (See Figure 8.1 for an illustration of this, based on a young person's guide to co-counselling.)

The healing that takes place when we discharge is as follows:

- a re-evaluation of our true selves
- fresh insight into the reality of our human nature
- increased awareness of how oppressive social and economic systems operate to the detriment of all people
- the opportunity to act on the previously obscured but now realised unlimited possiblities of our vision.

At the heart of the training is the belief that RC is a process that can be learned by anyone. Students learn how to re-discover their natural ability to give and get good attention from one another through basic listening skills. These skills are then used on a structured basis whereby, through mutual consent, people of all ages and backgrounds assist one another in co-counselling sessions to discharge confidentially and free themselves from the damaging effects of old hurts. During training, great emphasis is placed on confidentiality. This means that in classes and workshops no

Figure 8.1 How patterns of response develop (adapted by Ben Smith from Snyder, 1988)

one refers to anything anyone said in a counselling session or class.

As each group finishes a course they go into their tutor groups (11- to 13-year-olds) for one short session a week to teach the pupils listening and co-counselling skills and other activities and games to increase self-esteem. They offer them the option of being counselled on a one-to-one basis as well. I have set up support groups for all the student helpers to meet during lunch breaks and morning registration times every week. In these meetings we plan activities with tutor groups, celebrate successes and discuss problems, using co-counselling as a tool for helping each other.

Student helpers have been to every year assembly to tell them about the service. Often they were clapped spontaneously by the students. It was emphasised that no teacher would know about a student asking for counselling since it was a confidential service.

At first there were more student counsellors than there were students who requested counselling from a student helper. The service was publicised more and it has now become part of everyday life in the school. The younger students enjoy having the student helpers come to their tutor groups each week. Many stand in circles holding hands, telling "news and goods" and appreciating one another and themselves. They love the self-esteem games. It is having a knock-on effect in the school as a whole. The Year 7 pupils say that they really like having the student helper scheme because "it made us feel safe when we started in the school" and because it is reassuring "to know it is there and knowing that there is someone to talk to, even if we never actually use it". Photographs of the student helpers are displayed in every classroom. The younger pupils emphasise the usefulness of knowing what the student helpers look like since "we see who they are and it makes us more secure knowing there is someone there".

Increasing numbers of students have been coming forward to be counselled by the student helpers and me, and also to demand that action be taken if they are being bullied in any way.

The whole issue has been brought out into the open so that the focus is away from individuals. As a result, the climate in the school is safer and friendlier. In the past, when students were bullied, many of them saw the situation as a shameful individual problem, often blaming themselves and suffering in silence for fear of reprisals. This attitude is changing so that survivors of bullying take action to stop it recurring and bullies come to realise that they themselves have a problem which is causing their bullying behaviour. Both bullies and survivors are offered counselling and many take it up. Many volunteer to become student helpers themselves.

The peer helpers benefit too. They feel, justifiably, that they are taking positive action to contribute to the quality of life in their school community. Furthermore, they find that, through the process of counselling others, they get to know themselves more. They are mostly encouraged by the feedback from the tutor groups, but even when they have a difficult time with a group, the supervision sessions (where they share experiences with the other peer helpers) give them an invaluable opportunity to work through and overcome problems in a constructive, supportive environment. In the words of one of the helpers, "It encourages us. We can hear what other people are doing and then we know that other people are in the same boat and had bad feedbacks to start with as well and that they are getting over it." They learn too how important it is to listen to the criticisms when they come. For example, as three student helpers reflected:

Girl 1: We had a problem with our tutor groups to start with. The boys were very difficult.
Boy: It was a bad tutor group for the boys in the year and they had had a lot of problems with bullying.
Girl 1: And the girls didn't trust them to start with. And the girls said to their teacher, who said to us, that they didn't want to be counselled in a big group with the boys because they didn't trust them. They didn't want to talk about their own feelings in front of them 'cos they knew that the boys would laugh.
Girl 2: Now we counsel them in smaller groups and play a lot more games to get them all working together. And we pair boy/girl so that they can work together. We found that a lot more successful because when boys are in a big group they tend to ...
Boy: ... they just mess about.

The student helpers are clear about what they have gained from the experience. They say, "We gain in confidence" and "You learn to listen to people more – listen to their point of view and not be saying, 'No, no I don't agree'..." and "You realise there are other issues as well. Some things that people do they don't mean. It is just a cover-up for them."

What is valuable about our policy is the on-going process of it as much as the end results. It involves and empowers the students. Bullying is now talked about openly and regularly and everyone is aware that the whole school has a definition of bullying and that bullying behaviour is not acceptable. More survivors are coming forward to get it stopped; now when they ask for help, action is taken to stop it. Bullies also come forward to ask for help and are given it. In the school as a whole, many young people are learning how to co-counsel and this enables them to deal with many other problems they have in school.

Our next step is to conduct a survey of the student population to discover the extent to which bullying has been reduced and how far the climate of safety has been improved since we have been operating our anti-bullying policy.

CHAPTER 9

Peers Facing the Problem of Bullying in School

Derek Gillard

The purpose of this chapter is to describe how Marston Middle School is attempting to deal with the problem of bullying, in the hope that this may be useful to other schools and individuals. Having said this, it is vital to bear two points in mind. First, what we have done and are doing is appropriate to our particular circumstances – bullying in other schools and situations will vary both quantitatively and qualitatively and may therefore require different approaches – and second, the most important aspect of all our work has been the involvement of all concerned – staff and pupils – at all stages. For these two reasons, it would, in my view, be pointless for a school to feel that it could simply go through the processes which I outline here and hope to have dealt with the problem. I hope, however, that the issues discussed and the procedures described in this chapter will be of help to others in combatting what, for far too long, has caused misery for many of our pupils.

The school and its context

Marston Middle School lies on the north-east edge of the city of Oxford. The area is pleasant and varied, ranging from the picturesque village of Old Marston, through the 1930s semis and the developments of the 1950s to the smaller areas of newer housing. Rural Oxfordshire is minutes away to the north; Magdalen Bridge a mile or so to the south. The city centre is a ten-minute bus ride away (or a twenty-minute walk across the fields to the University parks).

The population is largely white, though there are residents from the ethnic minorities (mainly Asian, Chinese and African-Caribbean) and this mix is enriched by the presence of a small number of people from all over the world who come to the city to work or undertake research in the university or at the John Radcliffe Hospital which stands about a mile from the school.

The school began life in the late 1950s as a secondary modern school, becoming a middle school (for 9- to 13-year-olds) in the 1970s. In the early 1980s it was amalgamated with a nearby school, a move which caused great anxiety for the staffs of both schools and led to a level of bitterness and division which lasted many years. Today, the school has around 420 pupils, 20 teachers, pleasant, well-kept buildings and superb grounds. At the time of writing the school has suffered budget cuts which have resulted in the loss of three staff, causing significant reduction in the level of non-contact time.

Equal opportunities

I took up the post of headteacher in January 1989 and fairly quickly decided that my top priority had to be to improve the ethos of the school by tackling the problems caused by the poor relationships which were largely a hangover from the amalgamation. In the autumn term 1989 we made a start by introducing a personal and social education (PSE) programme for all pupils and by undertaking a project on equal opportunities. Working with the infant schools in the area, we asked the Equal Opportunities Unit at Westminster College to organise two days INSET for us. Teachers, education support staff, governors and parents were all involved and many issues were raised during these two days. Decisions were taken to set up a working party and to work towards agreeing an equal opportunities policy for the school.

Our work on bullying began at about the same time. There were three main reasons for this: first, there was bullying in the school – not a lot, I felt – but any bullying is undesirable, and if we were really going to tackle the ethos of the school and the quality of the relationships within it, we could not ignore this aspect of the problem. Second, there had been an increasing level of media interest in the problem of bullying: a programme on BBC2 and a number of articles and letters in the local and national press had recently appeared. And third, we saw it as an equal opportunities issue: pupils whose lives are being made miserable by bullying are not in a good position to take advantage of the social and educational opportunities offered by the school.

The bullying group

For all these reasons we set up a staff working party on bullying (known as the bullying group – though we tried not to bully!) in the latter half of the autumn term 1989. Seven members of staff volunteered and at their first meeting considered two issues:

1 How would we find out the extent and nature of bullying in the school?

2 Should we involve parents?

By the time the group met again two weeks later there had been articles on bullying in the Times Educational Supplement, the Observer and the Guardian. Clearly the issue was of great national concern.

The bullying group decided to invite the Neti-Neti Theatre Company to visit the school to perform their play *Only Playing Miss*. This had featured in two of the articles and was said to be a very powerful drama about bullying in schools. It also fitted well with our work on equal opportunities as it was performed in English, Bengali and Sign Language. We rang Neti-Neti and were disappointed that, because of the enormous media interest, they were booked up for months ahead. We did eventually get them to come and they were very well worth waiting for, but more of that later.

Personal and social education

The remainder of the December meeting was taken up with preparing a five-lesson programme on bullying for all pupils in their PSE lessons, with additional support in whole-school assemblies. The lessons, which took place in January 1990, began with a brainstorming session on "What is bullying?" and included class and group discussion on issues such as:

- what sort of people are bullies/victims?
- what sort of bullying is going on?
- where does bullying take place?
- what can we do about it?
- what should a school policy on bullying say?

During the lessons, pupils were asked to suggest a definition of bullying. We eventually agreed as a whole school that bullying was "any form of behaviour which causes unhappiness for another member of the school." I was personally delighted that we had arrived at such a broad definition with enormous implications for all of us – including me! It was significant that we used the term "member of the school": it does not apply only to pupils – teachers and support staff can be both bullies and bullied too. Since then we have modified our definition to include the word "deliberately" – since intentionality is very much part of bullying. We were guided to this conclusion by the booklet written by Tattum and Herbert (1990).

The bullying questionnaire

In March 1990 the bullying group met again to review the PSE lessons and decided that they had been successful in raising awareness of the issues. Several teachers from the school had attended a talk by Peter Smith in which the findings of the survey (Whitney and Smith, 1993) were presented, indicating that in the surveyed middle schools 11.6 per cent of pupils were bullied "sometimes" and 5.5 per cent "several times a week". So, the group decided that a questionnaire was the next step. Again, we were convinced that the important thing was to involve the pupils at all stages, so we prepared two further PSE lessons during which pupils were asked to devise their own questionnaire. The results of the work were collated and, at the end of April, the finished questionnaire was completed by all pupils during another PSE lesson. An instruction sheet for staff asked them to stress the confidential nature of the questionnaire: "No-one will even be able to identify your writing – you don't need to put anything but ticks!" This gave us a baseline of data from which to work; significantly, details of where and what sort of bullying was taking place and which year groups were most at risk.

The next meeting of the bullying group was in June 1990. This time, we invited our local police officer to join us and his contribution, together with that of a police inspector who was also a parent, was to prove invaluable.

The bully box

The Group agreed to set up a "bully box" as an attempt to deal with the problem that many children who are bullied are too nervous to tell someone about it. The box was to be like a ballot box, with a lockable lid. It would be positioned in the school library and there would be a supply of incident forms beside it. Any pupil who was being bullied but was too nervous to talk about it could write down the details on a form and put it in the box. At the end of each day, the box was to be emptied and the forms passed to an approriate member of staff for action.

The other major decision taken at that June meeting was to propose the setting up of a school bully court. Our co-opted police inspector was to attend a conference on bullying organised by Kidscape who were promoting the idea of school bully courts.

Finally, staff were asked to remind pupils that all bullying incidents must be reported and to be particularly vigilant about the times and places in which, according to the questionnaire results, most bullying was taking place.

The autumn term was one of great activity. The bully box was established in the library, Neti-Neti Theatre Company visited the school to perform *Only Playing Miss* and staff agreed to the setting up of the bully court.

The bully box was installed in September. At first many forms were filled – some of them were hoaxes or attempts to get other people into trouble. But we persevered and the number of forms submitted soon dwindled to a trickle and the hoaxes ceased.

The Neti-Neti Theatre Company's play was performed to the whole school in November and made a profound impact on staff and pupils. It is a powerful drama acted with minimal scenery and props.

The report from the Kidscape conference was also invaluable in helping us plan for our bully court. Founded by Michele Elliott, Kidscape publishes a wide range of material on bullying and other matters concerned with children's safety. Bully courts had been pioneered by Kidscape in a number of schools around the country; the first had been set up in response to pressure from pupils themselves.

The bully court

Further meetings of the bullying group in October and November 1990 were held to agree how the court would be established. It was decided that it should consist of twelve pupils – one to be elected by each class in the school. Again, PSE lessons were used as the vehicle for discussion about:

- the democratic process
- what a court is and how it operates
- the qualities needed by jury members

- the process of nominating candidates
- secret ballots.

In December, the first elections were held. Everything was done as officially as possible, with nomination forms and ballot papers typed and photocopied. The pupils responded well and eight boys and four girls were elected to serve as form representatives on the court. The gender imbalance suggested, however, that there was still much work to be done on equal opportunities.

The bullying group met in January 1991 and agreed a date for the inaugural meeting of the court. This was held at the end of January and discussed the rules and procedures of the court. My deputy and I were immensely impressed with the insights and common sense which the pupils brought to this meeting. As a result, a booklet was published setting out the court's rules and procedures.

Although we had decided right at the start not to involve parents in the early stages of this work, they had become progresssively more aware of it and, by this time, we were informing them in some detail through the half-termly school newsletter. All the comments we received were favourable.

Changes to the court

The court did not sit for six months after it was set up. This was not because there was no bullying in the school but because we made the decision at the start that only very serious cases would be dealt with by the court. Herein lay a problem: someone had to decide which cases the court could hear. In practice, when incidents were reported to me or to a member of staff, I tended to discuss the matter with that member of staff or with my deputy and we always agreed that the matter could be resolved without the court. I became progressively more concerned about this and so, after the first year, the rules were revised so that the decision as to whether a case should be heard was made by a group of four of the form representatives. This was an important change, taking power away from me and giving it to the pupils themselves – the principle which lies behind the whole concept of school bully courts. The result was that cases began to be heard.

The court sat to hear several cases of bullying in the following two years. On each occasion, we were immensely impressed by the sensible and sensitive way the members conducted their business. There was no sense of wielding power; rather, the members were at pains to point out to defendants that what they wanted to achieve was a more harmonious school in which all could get on with their work and with each other. Some cases were harder than others; in most, the defendant admitted guilt, in some, the defendant did not and the court had to try to assess the level of guilt. In all cases, members showed a willingness to be understanding but a resolve not to tolerate bullying. In some cases defendants cried; perhaps this was an indication that the court was taken seriously, but it also gave us some cause for concern – were we really just bullying the bullies?

Some pupils were anxious about the inevitable public nature of the court and felt that those who had been bullied might not want the problem aired in this forum – they might actually prefer the matter to be dealt with privately by, for example, a teacher. The members of the court discussed this and other problems at their half-termly business meetings and the rules and regulations were modified accordingly. For example, it was agreed that a friend could appear on behalf of a victim if the victim did not wish to appear.

The business meetings proved invaluable in themselves, not only because of the very sensible changes that were agreed to the procedure of the court, but as a forum for form representatives to report on known cases of bullying. The meetings were also excellent educationally, allowing pupils to serve as chair and clerk and encouraging them to discuss and debate.

A further change was made at the beginning of 1993 when it was agreed that bully court members should be left on their own to discuss any matters they saw fit, reporting to me at the end of the meeting. This has resulted in more incidents of bullying being discussed and dealt with. The proceedings became less formal; having identified a case of bullying, the court would send for the pupils and talk it through with them. If they couldn't resolve the matter themselves they would ask for the help of a member of staff, but in most cases they dealt with incidents themselves.

The no-blame approach

In 1993 the BBC's *That's Life* programme featured the work of a secondary school that was using the no-blame approach in dealing with bullying. The idea was to get bully and victim together with a member of staff to talk through what had been happening, to get the bully to understand and, if possible, to empathise with how the victim was feeling. The essence was not to blame anyone but to try to resolve problems. The court decided to try this approach so, instead of hearing cases in the formal court-like situation we had previously used, small groups of bully court members would talk through cases of bullying with bully and victim. This approach seems to work. Later in 1993 another programme showed the work of a London comprehensive school which was using peer counselling (see Chapter 10). This seemed to us to be a logical extension of the no-blame approach and we plan to try it for ourselves in the future.

Where are we now?

The members of the court have shown great sensitivity in dealing with cases but we have quickly become aware of a problem: the peer counselling approach requires training and the fact that the school elects a new bully court every autumn means that this training has to happen each year. We have not solved this problem yet. Our next task is to design a suitable training package for court members.

Members of the school – staff and pupils – feel that there is much less bullying than there used to be and that the quality of relationships in the school is now much better. Members of the court are themselves aware of issues surrounding punishment and blame, and are responsive to the evolving nature of our initiative. Questionnaire results indicate a reduction in levels of reported bullying. We have only just begun to tackle the problem. We certainly don't have all the answers yet – I doubt whether we ever will. The important thing is that we have acknowledged that the problem exists and are trying to do something about it.

CHAPTER 10

The Anti-Bullying Campaign (ABC) at Acland Burghley[1]

Hilary Paterson, Maggie Bentley, Franny Singer and Philip O'Hear

They (the students) are learning together a language of emotions to counteract the language of dominance and submission. (Victoria Neumark, TES)

What makes this scheme unique is that once the victim has talked the problem through, the bully is invited to a three-way discussion with the counsellor acting as arbiter. The scheme is such a success that aggressors are now coming forward of their own accord. (TV Times)

Bullying: the national and school context

In the last decade, the enormous and destructive impact of bullying in schools has become recognised. National government-sponsored research by the Psychology Department of the University of Sheffield (Smith and Sharp, 1994) has found that 25 per cent of school children experience being bullied during their school career. Ten per cent undergo physical threat, organised teasing, exclusion or harassment once a week or more. The research reveals that 4 per cent of school children admit to having bullied others. The research matches the adult memory of having coped at some time with the effects of bullying. This has led many to accept bullying as part of the toughening process by which we grow up. The Elton Report, Discipline in Schools (Elton, 1989) challenged this

[1]The national and international dissemination of this scheme was initially possible through the televised documentary on BBC2 in April 1994, screened as an educational special called *Bullying*. The public interest was so great that the school and the ABC team were unprepared for the impact. All efforts have been made to inform and advise other schools and educational establishments who have shown an interest. We are now very grateful for project development funding from the Calouste Gulbenkian Foundation, the Paul Hamlyn Foundation and Timeplan, and also to Brian Lee of Multimedia Exhibitions.

view. Not only is bullying widespread, its effects are corrosive and long-term, and pose major threats to educational success and social cohesion. Kidscape, the national child safety charity, has demonstrated a link between childhood bullying behaviour and later crime, whilst work by Sheffield University, the Gulbenkian Foundation, the DFE and others shows bullying to be a significant factor in school truancy, underachievement, dropping-out, unhappiness and depression.

The research shows that bullying occurs in a cyclical pattern in which humiliation, aggression and violence are spread. A bully has always been a victim first and bullying is learned as a way of hiding or disguising this, as the pain is perceived as being too much to confront. Bullying is the projection of unwanted parts of the self on to another in order for that other to carry away the shame, fear, humiliation and guilt from the originator. This of course brings only temporary relief since the unresolved internal feelings still exist in the bully. Consequently, the bullying will continue and often intensify until it is challenged and resolved.

This cycle needs to be broken and painful feelings confronted, otherwise the bullying can appear to go when suppressed but will reappear in another and usually more distorted form. It causes misery, distress, illness, underachievement and criminal behaviour. This is accepted in many institutions as part of the culture and experience of life. Acland Burghley School does not accept this because it sees the damage done to children from an early age. Acland Burghley School is committed to improving the quality of life for its students and promoting new values of community and self-respect in its code of conduct.

Early anti-bullying work at Acland Burghley

Acland Burghley in Camden, London, already enjoyed a reputation in 1989 as a happy, secure and open school. Despite this, inept handling of a parental report of a girl being bullied drove the problem behaviour underground and left the victim completely isolated. When it recurred, she attempted suicide. In response to this, the Chair of Governors linked Acland Burghley with Sheffield University in 1990, and persuaded Camden LEA to pay for the University's survey of bullying.

Acland Burghley was one of the first London schools to take part in the survey. This was carried out in March 1991, preceded and followed by two half-day training sessions for staff. Thirteen per cent of Acland Burghley students reported having been bullied, less than the average for South Yorkshire urban secondary schools but more than the whole-survey average of 10 per cent. Much of the reported bullying took the form of name-calling. Fewer pupils than usual had told teachers and one third of students had told no one. On the positive side, 41 per cent of students responded that they tried to help victims of bullying and over 50 per cent said that they could neither understand nor accept bullying and they would not join in. The survey project staff noted that "it may be possible to mobilise peer group opinion further against bullying".

Maggie Bentley, the deputy head, and students worked from this starting point to lead whole-school work against bullying. The newly-launched student council conducted another survey among students to identify more explicitly their perceptions of what constituted bullying and what action would be taken to prevent it. A draft anti-bullying policy was developed for further consultation with staff (teaching and support staff) and parents (through the school's annual Parents' Day). From this student-led work, an anti-bullying policy was developed and adopted by governors in June 1992.

Acland Burghley's anti-bullying policy

The anti-bullying policy was the first to be adopted by a Camden school. It was ahead of the later government and LEA exhortations to schools to adopt such policies. The students' definition of bullying and the steps they describe for tackling it are as follows.

a) What is a bully?
A bully is someone who physically or verbally hurts someone.
A bully is someone who likes to be in control of other people.
A bully can be a girl, a boy, a man or a woman.
A bully usually picks on people who cannot defend themselves.
Bullying happens in many different forms but a clear definition is:
"It is the wilful, conscious desire to hurt, threaten or frighten someone."

b) What kind of things are bullying behaviour?
Verbal abuse, stealing, physical abuse, threatening and blackmail are all forms of bullying behaviour.
Being racist and sexist can be called bullying.
The bully usually sees the hurt he or she has caused as a joke.
Making someone feel inferior is bullying.
The term "bullying" covers a very wide range of possible situations.
Name-calling, teasing, stealing, abuse of any kind are all forms of bullying. A bully uses THREAT AND FEAR as weapons.

c) What should happen to bullies?
Bullying is wrong and if anyone is bullying they should get punished. There are different levels of bullying. This should be taken into account when deciding on a punishment. A possible plan of punishment is:

1 interview with teacher
2 letter home
3 suspension/exclusion
4 expulsion/permanent exclusion.

Acland Burghley School does not want to resort to step 4, but a bully's victim(s) must be protected and if this protection can only come from the removal of the bully, then so be it. Some bullies need the type of help that Acland Burghley cannot provide.
Bullying must be identified and steps taken to prevent it. After all, prevention is better than cure.

d) What should happen to the victim?
The victim will need to talk to someone about how they feel once the bullying has stopped. An organised discussion between the bully and the victim could help to show how the victim feels.

The second survey and the start of intervention

As a result of this work much more bullying was reported to staff who were now, owing to the policy, able to respond with greater sensitivity and consistency. In March 1993, Sheffield University undertook a second survey as part of the DFE-funded research into the effects of intervention. This survey result was encouraging. A reduction of 21.8 per cent had occurred in students reporting being bullied and a reduction of 37.5 per cent in those reporting taking part in bullying. Nonetheless, 10 per cent of the school still reported experiencing bullying and 3.5 per cent reported bullying others. Name-calling in class remained the most common form of bullying and, once again, only about half of the instances of bullying resulted in effective intervention by staff whilst students' disapproval of bullying remained high.

Thus although 73 per cent of students felt bullying had reduced and that effective action had been taken, the second survey showed that a level of bullying remained that largely went unnoticed by, and unreported to, staff.

Maggie Bentley also stayed in contact with the Sheffield University project and explored a variety of models of intervention. Maggie focussed on student-centred schemes and, in particular, the peer counselling scheme at Chaucer School in Sheffield which she and a group of students had visited. In the light of this consultation, she undertook to launch a similar scheme at Acland Burghley. With support from volunteer staff at school and from Camden's Education Social Work Service, Maggie recruited and trained the first cohort of counsellors. Their brief, like that of the counsellors on the Chaucer School scheme, was to offer support and advice for victims, helping them to develop or choose strategies for resisting or reporting the bullying they experienced.

Within weeks of the scheme starting, the counsellors faced the limitations of this approach and, in their supervision meetings, challenged Maggie to widen their brief. Without approaching the bully and seeking to intervene, the counsellors believed their work would remain peripheral or, worse, simply act as a reporting system to staff. If it became the latter, they argued, it would serve no function since the victim clients were presenting themselves to the counselling system precisely because they were reluctant to seek adult/staff help.

ABC is born

Maggie Bentley took a huge risk. She allowed the Acland Burghley student counsellors to offer an intervention and mediation service. She took on herself the burden of providing training through the weekly supervision meetings. The uniqueness of the Acland Burghley peer counselling scheme is to be found in this courageous decision to trust and empower one set of young people to offer, in a non-hierarchical way, the opportunity for profound change to other young people locked in the roles of victim and bully. Resting both on the residual peer culture against bullying found in the first survey, and on the determined adult (staff and parent) stance and action against any kind of discriminatory behaviour, this decision became a wholly successful reality. The sensitive filming of the early work of the pilot ABC project by Windfall Films and its screening in April 1994 on BBC2 has led to an enormous national and international interest in the scheme, its principles and its method of working.

How the ABC pilot scheme works

The principles and targets of the scheme are defined as follows. ABC (the anti-bullying campaign) is a confidential service where students might feel more willing and less threatened to discuss their problems in a non-hierarchical way. (This peer group approach has proved so far to be very successful and has attracted a wide range of students, including many involved in active bullying.) ABC also creates the opportunity for a personal learning experience for a broad spectrum of students, helping them to cooperate and coordinate and to deal with conflict in a safe and positive environment. It empowers the students, which in turn benefits the school with the introduction of a new awareness and positivity to its community.

ABC is student-led and student-managed. All students (Years 7-11) are given the opportunity to be selected for training as a counsellor. Application forms are freely available to anyone who wishes to be considered for this scheme.

Applicants pass through three separate selection panels, one of which is a student body, before a final shortlist is drawn up. Each panel has its own criteria and any applicant who is unsuccessful is kept on file pending re-selection. Selected counsellors are then trained for two days at the beginning of the school year before becoming active in the counselling rota, which lasts for six weeks in each of two terms.

There are also a number of administrative commitments that the counsellor has to fulfil as part of the overall responsibility for running ABC: these include reception duty, assemblies, weekly meeting agenda, chairing weekly meetings, updating information board, case debriefing, organising outside visits, participation in outside visits, media appearances and interviews, home preparation and telephone time. Students are supervised by the coordinator and four other teachers on a weekly basis, in small groups, pairs or individually.

There is an appointment and rota system whereby clients are accommodated as quickly as possible (although emergency appointments may be made on an ad hoc basis). The service operates during the lunch hour three days per week. Currently there are four counsellors on duty during any one session, two in reception and two in active counselling. Student clients seeking assistance are self-referred and an individual session is scheduled for ten minutes, although this time is not fixed and will be extended when necessary or a further appointment made. Clients and counsellors negotiate together how many sessions may be required.

The six-weekly counselling rota must be flexible enough to

accommodate the possibility of a large and complex case emerging that necessitates a re-scheduling of the rota. Counsellors carrying a caseload may be taken off the rota if it is felt necessary; this decision is negotiated with the coordinator.

There is a confidentiality and safety contract between the client and the counsellor explained at the outset. The session is completely confidential and will not be referred to anyone else unless:

- the case is of too serious a nature (e.g. life-threatening or revealing abuse or having child protection implications);
- the case involves personal issues or personal friends that the counsellor feels will bias the outcome.

If the case is referred on, it can involve the active support of the initial counsellor if the client so wishes.

A new client will be allocated a counsellor by the rota coordinator after arriving at reception. After the first session, the counsellor has to decide whether or not to continue managing a case. The client and counsellor decide together whether to continue the sessions, to close the case or refer on.

If the case is of a simple nature involving one-to-one counselling, the counsellor will listen, suggest strategies and generally facilitate the client's own problem-solving skills in developing a plan of action. If the case necessitates contact with a third party or parties, e.g. a teacher or teachers, the counsellor may initially suggest that the client sets up a meeting with the counsellor's support. If the case involves other students, time is given for a strategy to develop, and the counsellor may contact the other students confidentially, inviting them to a group discussion in the presence of a mediating counsellor.

Whatever the nature of the case, there is always the opportunity to discuss it anonymously in supervision, unless it falls into a category outside the confidentiality and safety contract.

At the end of a case, a simple quantitative data sheet is filled out so that a cumulative record can be kept of the nature of cases passing through ABC.

Key issues arising from ABC

Major developments are needed to enable us to tackle nine severe problems faced by ABC. Mostly these result from its success and huge impact inside and outside the school.

1 Huge responsibility is given to students trained as counsellors, who need considerable on-going support. As the scheme grows, investment in good supervision, debriefing and training is absolutely essential.

2 Time for counselling sometimes necessitates students missing important curriculum time. ABC meetings also conflict with other work of the school. Time management, investment in good coordination and the training and maintenance of a large pool of counsellors helps alleviate this problem.

3 Confidentiality and record keeping can conflict. A good administrator keeps the boundaries clear and keeps records solely for the purpose of quantitative data.

4 Counsellors can become overburdened and experience "burn out". This is very undesirable and can be counteracted by having a large pool of available trained counsellors, together with access to professional training and debriefing to supplement the staff and peer supervision/advice.

5 Counsellors at times are faced with difficult cases or find a case becomes unmanageable. An administrator sets out clear guidelines in a job description and the coordinator assists in referring such cases on.

6 The demands of school students for help from the scheme, together with the external interest, has created great difficulties in completing formal evaluation of the scheme. This is, of course, essential before development proposals are finalised for implementation. Adequate staff and purchase of external evaluation are both essential if we are to identify and institutionalise the key elements of the pilot responsible for its success.

7 Because of wide interest in this scheme and the keenness of other schools to pilot their own, students and other staff have been involved in travelling out of school. This is expensive in both travel costs and time. In-house workshops have been organised which cut down the need to travel out and ensure that dissemination is cost-effective.

8 The national and international interest in the scheme, whilst very encouraging and stimulating, has created a huge amount of work in sending out information and in dealing with personal enquiries. The development of a full training pack would meet most of this demand in an effective and manageable way, supplemented by school-based workshops. This proposal of course has considerable time and cost implications.

9 As a result of the media interest and the exposure of young students to the motives of journalists and reporters, it has been necessary to draft a protection code and a checklist so that the essential integrity of the scheme is not jeopardised in any way by commercial or other non-educational motives. The school is firm in its beliefs that this scheme must stay within the control of its students and not be abused or misrepresented. The time-consuming work involved here is all being done voluntarily and now requires paid administration.

The effects of the ABC

The scheme has created the opportunity to challenge traditional and stereotypical ideas about problem solving. It helps the students come to grips with their real situation with all its demands, difficulties and pressures and it creates a sense of responsibility through discussion and negotiation. It offers a non-hierarchical structure in which to contribute to the school community. Every opportunity is taken to give students full involvement in project development. This is part of the whole-school commitment to collective effort. Counsellors, who have been chosen from all backgrounds and include previous bullies and students whose record of work or behaviour is poor, have developed hugely. They show significantly increased articulateness, social skills, confidence with peers and adults and, above all, they benefit from a sense of real achievement and real responsibility. Some counsellors who seemed at risk of dropping out of school have become positively integrated into school.

Clients (both victims and bullies) have achieved productive solutions to the problems they face, or at least some of them. They have been able to use confidential, safe and non-hierarchical space to explore the feelings arising from and contributing to their role as victim or bully. Along with the counsellors, they are the most committed advocates of the ABC scheme and many have since applied to work for it.

The impact on the school of both the work of the scheme and the positive changes it has supported in counsellors and the clients cannot be overstated. As the first programme of its kind in the UK to use mediation and not confrontation, it has encouraged students to find strategies for change, not just in personal bullying situations but more generally. This sense of achievement and responsibility empowers students, unlocking much of the potential of the school community. It has helped establish a bond of enormous trust between students and staff. The scheme has had a huge external impact which has been welcome, and has imposed an enormous demand on counsellors, volunteer staff and the school as a whole.

Part III

Peer Counselling and Support: Evaluating its Impact

CHAPTER 11

Evaluating Peer Counselling in Your Own Setting

The evaluation strategies which we present in this chapter can give all participants the opportunity to reflect on their own learning, to be more aware of the processes which are happening among their fellow counsellors and to monitor the changes which are taking place over time in the school as a result of their interventions. The evaluation strategies can also be used as a resource for being constructively critical about aspects of the peer counselling service where change might be beneficial, for example in the selection of peer helpers, the nature and extent of training and supervision, the decision-making powers of the pupil participants, and so on. In this sense, evaluation is an essential part of the learning process involved in relating more creatively and positively to people in one's own school community.

Evaluation strategies are bound to vary according to the needs and contexts within which the peer counselling is taking place. It is our view that evaluation which will enhance the whole experience of peer counselling is likely to happen in circumstances where there is:

- a climate of trust and genuine enquiry;
- a willingness on the part of adults and students to engage in a cooperative approach to evaluation from which all benefit;
- honesty about the reasons for the evaluation as an integral part of the peer counselling service from the beginning;
- fostering of constructive criticism rather than a destructive judgemental stance.

In this chapter, we make some suggestions. This is not an exhaustive list but rather a set of guidelines which may be adapted by participants to suit their own requirements.

Observation

There are times when it is helpful to have external perspectives on aspects of the peer counselling service. A person sympathetic to the aims and ideals of a particular project could be invited to observe different aspects of the service. This observer could, for example, be invited to sit in on a training session and give feedback to the group on what they saw. With the permission of participants and respecting the confidential nature of the material under discussion, the observer could comment on such aspects of training as:

- what appeared to be happening in the group?
- which aspects of a training exercise appeared to be challenging?
- who spoke and who did not?
- how was silence used?
- were there gender differences in response to the exercises?

The observer could then reflect these perceptions back to the training group and share in the discussion which arose. It would be most useful if one participant was nominated as scribe to note the observations and the issues which emerged in discussion.

Diaries

Most peer counsellors will be involved in a project for quite a long period of time. The project facilitator can encourage them to keep diaries in which they record:

- reflections on the skills which they acquired during training;
- reflections on what they learned from supervision;
- new ways in which they are relating to others;
- how they respond to their clients;
- problems which they encounter in the role of peer counsellor and how, if at all, they are resolved.

These diary commentaries can be discussed in supervision groups. Common issues which recur can be stored as records of the life of the peer counselling initiative.

Checklists

Each cohort of trainees can be encouraged to develop its own criteria for evaluating development as counsellors. These can be used for an on-going monitoring of progress or for overall evaluation of the group performance at set times, for example during skills training. Sample checklists, such as those following, give an idea of the range of possibilities.

Learning new skills

1 What is the most important skill which I learned during this training session?

2 How well did I learn it?

3 How confident do I feel about using this skill?

4 What is my next step in using this skill?

5 Any further comments?

Dynamics of the training group

1 Who contributed to this discussion?

2 Who did not contribute to this discussion?

3 Was the atmosphere of the group cooperative or competitive (or other)?

4 How were difficulties received in the training group?

5 Were there conflicts among members of the group? If yes, how, if at all, were they resolved?

6 Any other issues?

Feelings and reactions to a training session

1 How did I feel?

2 Did I feel frustrated with the others?

3 Did I feel frustrated with myself?

4 Was I afraid of looking silly?

5 Did I find it hard not to talk?

6 Did I follow the instructions?

7 Were there any difficulties in carrying out the tasks?

Self-evaluation

1 Did I work well in my group?
2 Did I help someone in my group?
3 Did I help the group as a whole?
4 Did I listen to my partner?
5 Did I like the activity?
6 Did I have enough time?
7 Were there any other issues?

Brainstorming common problems

During training, participants in small groups can brainstorm difficulties which they fear they may encounter once they begin their peer support work. Within their groups, they brainstorm the question, "What do I do if ...?" The questions posed by each person are recorded without comment by a scribe. They then form the basis for further training. An example from one "What if?" brainstorm is given in Chapter 4. Here is an example of pupils from Marston Middle School brainstorming the costs and benefits of being members of the bully court.

Positive things
It is a quality not to be unfair.
Being more mature.
Bullies are insecure – so we feel more secure.
We learn how to deal with it better.
It helps you in everyday life.
Being more mature and not being a bully.
To be more understanding of feelings.
About what people are like.
Help to understand people better.
Understand people.

They are also aware of some difficulties:

Drawbacks
It is hard sometimes when they won't talk.
When people go on about things. Like they tell a story and then change things in it.
It is hard to deal with but it is a challenge.
I don't like people who lie.

We sometimes get put under pressure from other kids. You can get their friends into trouble. So you have to say, "This is the right thing to do."
Pressure and stress. You have to be strong inside yourself. They can give you a bad look. I have to go and talk about this with close friends. My friends talk about it.
I would like a support group.
It is difficult when your friends are bullied. You are more close to them so it is difficult.

Facts and figures

It is extremely useful to have a database of information, for example recording the number of clients who come for counselling, their age, gender, the kinds of problems they present. A simple coding system can be devised for each peer counsellor to make a routine record of the information. No names of clients should be used in order to safeguard confidentiality. Figure 11.1 gives an example of a frequency distribution of calls to a telephone counselling service. This group of peer counsellors also kept a record (Figure 11.2) of the types of problems which the clients presented to their counsellors; the information was broken down by gender.

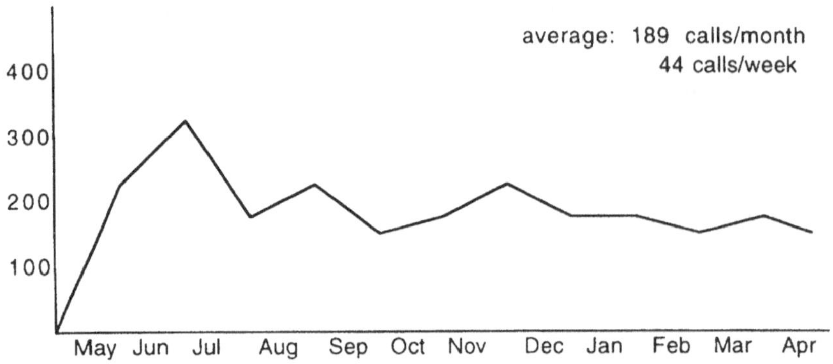

Figure 11.1 Number of calls per month to the Teen Line peer telephone listening service (adapted from Boehm *et al.*, 1991)

Another strategy might be to make a record of behaviour in the playground before and after the introduction of the interventions: for example, the number of fights during selected breaktimes in the months before and after a conflict resolution programme was begun.

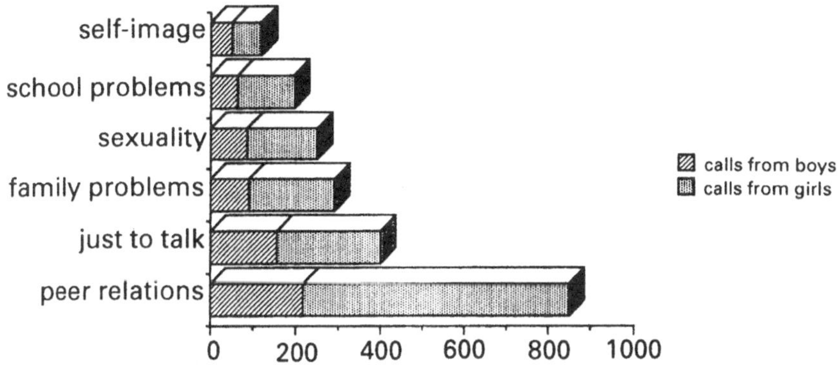

Figure 11.2 Reasons for phoning a peer telephone service, split by gender

Video

Video recordings of peers counselling one another during training can make an invaluable basis for self-evaluation. Care must be taken that they are used supportively and that all comments, even critical ones, are given constructively. Playback is best done in a small training group with an adult facilitator present. The video can be paused at significant moments in the interaction, preferably at points selected by the participants themselves. Questions which can be asked include:

What was happening for you at that moment?

What thoughts were going through your mind?

How do you think X (the client) felt at that moment?

What strategies did you have then?

What effect did you think it had on X?

Did X expect anything of you at that point?

Parallel questions can be asked of the client, so deepening the peer counsellors' insights into the counselling process. Interpersonal Process Recall (IPR), described in Chapter 4, is a powerful method for facilitating self-reflection and evaluation. Recordings are deleted at the end of the session to ensure confidentiality.

Questionnaires

Questionnaires can be used to establish a baseline before the intervention begins and then to record predicted or expected changes which may have taken place. The *My Life in School* questionnaire (Arora, 1989) is widely used to assess levels of bullying in schools.

Measuring bullying with the *My Life in School* checklist

About the checklist

The checklist describes different things which might happen to a pupil in school during any one week. About half of these things are nice or neutral things and about half are more unpleasant. This mixture is deliberate. It draws attention away from bullying. The checklist has three special features:

Flexibility

The checklist exists in many different versions. The main variations are to do with wording, the inclusion of particular items or whether pupils are expected to put their names on it or not. You can change the checklist to meet the needs of your school. If you do change it, make sure you include an equal proportion of positive and negative items. If you wish to calculate the bullying or general aggression index you will need to keep in items 4, 8, 10, 24, 37 and 39.

An indirect but more precise measurement of bullying

The checklist avoids the direct question "Are you being bullied?" This question is avoided because:

- There are so many different kinds of bullying behaviour.
- Children can define bullying in different ways.
- The word "bullying" can be emotive and pupils may not answer honestly.

Reference to the immediate past

The pupil is asked to report only on those events which happened during the past week. Memories of events occuring more than one week ago can be inaccurate. For very young pupils, you may want to ask what happened to them the day before or even today.

Box 11.1 The My Life in School questionnaire

I am a boy	☐	I am a girl	☐
Age	☐	Year	☐

During this week in school another child:	Not at all	Once	More than once
1 Called me names.			
2 Said something nice to me.			
3 Was nasty about my family.			
4 Tried to kick me.			
5 Was very nice to me.			
6 Was unkind because I am different.			
7 Gave me a present.			
8 Said they'd beat me up.			
9 Gave me some money.			
10 Tried to make me give them money.			
11 Tried to frighten me.			
12 Asked me a stupid question.			
13 Lent me something.			
14 Stopped me playing a game.			
15 Was unkind about something I did.			
16 Talked about clothes with me.			
17 Told me a joke.			
18 Told me a lie.			
19 Got a gang on me.			
20 Tried to make me hurt other people.			
21 Smiled at me.			
22 Tried to get me into trouble.			
23 Helped me carry something.			
24 Tried to hurt me.			
25 Helped me with my class work.			
26 Made me do something I didn't want to do.			
27 Talked about TV with me.			
28 Took something off me.			
29 Shared something with me.			
30 Was rude about the colour of my skin.			
31 Shouted at me.			

32 Played a game with me.			
33 Tried to trip me up.			
34 Talked about things I like.			
35 Laughed at me horribly.			
36 Said they would tell on me.			
37 Tried to break something of mine.			
38 Told a lie about me.			
39 Tried to hit me.			

What information can the checklist give?

Using the checklist will provide the following information:

- A *bullying index*
- A *general aggression index*
- A comprehensive picture of "Life in School"
- A means of identifying bullied pupils
- Any extra information you want (by putting your own questions in).

Administering the checklist

Introducing the checklist

Give the pupils some explanation about why they are being presented with the questionnaire. This can be fairly general, for example, "We would like to know what happens to people in school. In this booklet are various things that might have happened to you during the last week."

Read out at least the first item for the pupils and show them how to complete this. You can read out each item if you prefer. If there are children with a reading age below 8 years, they may need individual assistance.

Achieving the right atmosphere

Make sure the pupils are working individually and that their work cannot be seen by other pupils. There should be no discussion between pupils whilst the checklist is being completed. Give each pupil as much privacy as possible.

Scoring the bullying/general aggression index

To establish levels of bullying, the checklist can be scored to provide a bullying index and general aggression index. Subsequently you can repeat the checklist after you have intervened, using it like a "dipstick" to find out whether or not your anti-bullying strategies are working. You will probably see a reduction in the general aggression index before the bullying index comes down.

Use the bullying index with groups of 40 pupils or more. For groups smaller than 40 it will not be sufficiently reliable to allow valid comparisons. If you only have small classes, you can calculate the bullying index for the whole school.

The key items for identifying levels of bullying
Item 4: Tried to kick me
Item 8: Said they'd beat me up
Item 10: Tried to make me give them money
Item 24: Tried to hurt me
Item 37: Tried to break something of mine
Item 39: Tried to hit me.

The responses to these items will give a quick impression of the extent of bullying in your school.

The bullying index
Step One: For each of the six items, count the number of times that a tick was placed under the category "more than once". Do this separately for each of the six key items.
Step Two: Divide the scores for each separate item by the number of checklists completed. This will give you the percentage of pupil responses for each item.
Step Three: Add all the six percentages.
Step Four: Divide this number by six. Use two decimal places, e.g. 7.12 or 8.03. This figure is the bullying index for your school.

The general aggression index
Step One: For each of the six items, count the number of times that a tick was placed under the category "more than once". Do this separately for each of the six key items.
Step Two: Divide the scores for each separate item by the number of checklists completed. This will give you the percentage of pupil responses for each item.
Step Three: For each of the six items, count the number of times that a tick was placed under the category "once". Do this separately for each of the six key items.
Step Four: Divide the scores for each separate item by the number of checklists completed. This will give you the percentage of pupil responses for each item.
Step Five: Add all the twelve percentages.

Step Six: Divide this number by twelve. Use two decimal places, e.g. 15.02 or 20.55. This figure is the general aggression index for your school.

Interpreting the results: gender differences

Boys' responses are normally around two or three times as high as girls' responses. This does not necessarily mean that boys are bullied more often than girls. Acts of bullying include a wide variety of behaviours, from very clear physical aggression to more subtle threats of this and on to psychological intimidation, demeaning, social exclusion etc. Not all these items are included in the checklist. The six items do have a bias towards more physical bullying. Consequently, bullying of boys may be detected more easily with the index than that of girls. However, physical and non-physical bullying usually co-exist, so a high bullying index can be interpreted as indicating the likelihood of a high level of bullying all round and vice versa.

For the same reasons, girls who are bullied may not be as readily identified with the six items alone. Item 35, "Laughed at me horribly" or Item 38, "Told a lie about me" can provide useful information for identifying more indirect bullying.

Using the checklist to build a comprehensive picture of life in your school

You may wish to look at all the actions on the checklist to obtain a more all-round picture of what happens in school during one week. You can also assess the experiences of individual pupils or small groups of pupils in this way. For the small groups you can work out the percentages of responses to each item on the checklist for each of the two categories "once" and "more than once".

Using the checklist to identify bullied pupils

Any pupil who ticks any of the key items under "more than once" is more at risk of being bullied. If you want to find out who is being bullied you will need to ask the pupils to put their names on the checklist before they fill it in. This may make some pupils more reluctant to give honest answers.

Using the checklist to gain extra information of your choice

You can use the back page to find out any extra information you feel is important. This might be general information about the pupil, their perceptions of the school or more information about their experience. Make sure that this page can be completed both by pupils who are bullied and by pupils who are not to avoid drawing attention to the bullied group.

Copyright

There is no copyright on the checklist. Tiny Arora would however appreciate:

- A copy of any results you have obtained by using the checklist;
- A copy of any different version of the checklist which you have made.

Any information received will be treated as confidential. Tiny's address is:

Division of Education
University of Sheffield
388 Glossop Road
Sheffield S10 2JA.

Interviews

It may not be possible to interview all who are involved in a peer counselling project, but selected interviews can illuminate the processes which particular individuals are experiencing. This material can enhance any report of the project which is being written and can highlight key issues of concern. This extract from an interview conducted by Helen Cowie with Duncan and Sarah, Year 8 pupils at Marston Middle School, gives insights into the strategies which they use in their peer support work and some of the difficulties which they face. These peer counsellors are also demonstrating some of the ethical dilemmas which they face as they discuss the issue of the punishment of those who bully others.

S: We talk to the victim and the bully separately.
D: We use the soft approach. We are not too pushy. We talk it over and try to get them to be friends. It doesn't always work. We give advice, like keep away from each other. Eighty per cent don't bother each other again. Twenty per cent are more difficult. Some are going to be bullies all their lives. We hand them over to Mr Gillard. The 80 per cent we can deal with ourselves.
S: We ask if they still want to go ahead. If yes, we speak to them on their own. We ask the victim questions like "When? Why? Is it over?", then we pull in the bully and talk to them and then, if they both want, we talk with them together. The victim gets very emotional sometimes and cries. The bully ignores our questions and does not react. The expression is as if they hadn't

done anything. That's why we talk to them separately first. It gives the victim more confidence. I speak from my own experience. I try – I know people who have been bullied.
D: You give advice – "Stay away if you can't be friends. Speak to one another – it needn't be on a friendly basis (i.e. you don't need to be best friends)." Then call in the bully and give some advice. Then together – both agree to get along. Most of the time it's not that serious – some name-calling, then it goes away. The serious things go to Mr Gillard.
HC: Any failures?
S: No.
D: We don't really. Not big ones. Some things don't come to the bully court. We only deal with what we get.
HC: Any drawbacks?
D: People think "What can you do? You can't punish them." We lack power.
S: But it's not fair to hand out punishment. You could do it to people you don't like.

This kind of material can be extremely useful for planning further training and for evaluating the benefits of an intervention.

Surveys

It is important to have some method for evaluating client satisfaction. It is, of course, essential to ensure that the confidentiality of the client/counsellor relationship is maintained. However, provided that it is carried out discreetly and with sensitivity, it is possible to have a follow-up survey to assess the helpfulness or otherwise of the counselling and support which was offered. It would be very time-consuming to follow up everyone, but a sample of, say, every tenth client who attended the service could be selected. Alternatively, a random sample of all pupils at the school or of all pupils in a particular year group could provide useful information about pupil satisfaction with the service.

There have been two evaluation studies of bully courts. Brier and Ahmad (1991) assessed the impact of a bully court on a middle school in Sheffield by using pre- and post-intervention questionnaire surveys. They found that there was a reasonable reduction in levels of bullying in classes which had been involved in the bully court. In other classes which had not been involved levels of bullying remained unchanged. Brier and Ahmad point out that extensive curriculum work had been undertaken with the intervention classes which extended beyond the bully court itself. It was not possible to identify whether the change in levels of bullying was due to the bully court alone. Pitfield (1992) gave questionnaires to students in Marston School who had been involved in the bully courts. The students felt that there had been a positive impact on bullying in school but not so much outside school. They also felt that peer attitudes towards bullying had improved. Pitfield went on to carry out a survey of teacher and student attitudes towards bully courts. She found that students were more positive about bully courts than teachers, mostly agreeing that "It is good that some children have the power to give a punishment to another member of their form" and that "With a bully court, bullies would not bully so much because they would be scared of going to court." In contrast, teachers felt that the court would have little influence on bullying behaviour.

CHAPTER 12

How Do We Know It Works?

The need for evaluation

As we have seen in the first two sections of this book, there has been a considerable upsurge in the number of programmes of peer counselling and support. Almost without exception, the schools view these projects in a positive light. It is generally acknowledged that the school benefits, the ethos improves, the young people's distress is alleviated and the peer counsellors themselves gain in self-esteem, confidence and maturity. However, these judgements tend to be made subjectively and there is a growing sense, not only in the research community but also amongst practitioners and peer counsellors, of the need for systematic and rigorous evaluations of both process and outcome if we are to identify the factors which facilitate the successful development of a peer counselling programme and, just as importantly, its implementation over time.

One of the difficulties is that the practitioners are usually so busy implementing the programme that there is little time left for systematic evaluation of the effectiveness of what they are doing. Furthermore, through their commitment to the programme, there is a danger that they may overlook flaws in its design. A number of researchers, notably de Rosenroll (1989), suggest that we need to be cautious about concluding that peer help programmes are being properly used and that they are being systematically evaluated. They recommend that those who set up peer counselling programmes should also involve experts in research methods so that a proper evaluation can be carried out. While anecdotal accounts by participants in the projects are useful up to a point, there is a real danger that some programmes fail to evaluate the effectiveness of their work adequately and that subjective comments become the only type of evaluation which occurs.

Research strategies

One common research design uses the *pre- post-test method* in which the evaluator tries to discover if some change has taken place during the implementation of the programme. Researchers have, for example, measured changes in the self-concept of the peer counsellors over the period of time in which they are selected and trained, acquire experience in the role of peer counsellor and learn to share common concerns in a supervision group. Standardised instruments are often appropriate, though it may be necessary to devise new ones sensitive to the subtle changes over time which take place. A system can be devised so that the peer helpers can collect information on how many clients they have seen and on what kinds of problems are presented to them. It is also possible to measure outcomes through questionnaire studies or by consulting records of, for example, bullying incidents and whether the numbers of these have dropped since the implementation of the peer support intervention.

Schools often introduce peer support services as part of a response to an identified social need such as tackling bullying or drug abuse, or promoting inclusive education for students with physical or educational difficulties. Evaluation of the effectiveness of their overall programmes may include measures to identify a reduction of an undesirable behaviour or an increase in an appropriate behaviour. A peer support service by itself is unlikely to reduce bullying or drug abuse. It may, however, affect social awareness and improve the overall ethos of the school as a community. How can this be measured? Eslea and Smith (1995) looked specifically at the impact which an anti-bullying programme implemented in four primary schools had on social attitudes to bullying. Student responses to three questionnaire items were compared over time: pre-intervention in 1990, immediately post-intervention in 1992 and a year later in 1993. The items asked students:

a. whether or not they would help someone who was being bullied;
b. whether or not they could join in bullying someone;
c. whether or not they were upset by others being bullied.

Eslea and Smith found a consistent increase in positive social attitudes in all four schools, regardless of whether or not levels of bullying had changed. A similar follow-up study in secondary schools has recently been conducted by Thompson and Sharp (in preparation). Similarly, although levels of bullying behaviour have scarcely changed, social responsibility for tackling bullying behaviour has continued to increase in schools where it has been encouraged. More students than ever before were willing to help a peer who was being bullied and were less ready to join in. The findings of these two studies suggest that evaluation of the effectiveness of interventions such as peer counselling should include data about social attitudes and responsibility. If the evaluation in these studies had only related to levels of bullying, then students, parents and staff would have seen no evidence of the impact of their efforts over time.

Many schools in the UK are annually involved in the screening of students so that they can measure the extent of their progress. Such screening has commonly become known as assessing "value added". Whilst much of this screening relates to attainment and aptitude, it would be so easy to include a few questions relating to social attitude and responsibility. Here are examples of such questions:

If someone in your class was obviously upset, would you:
- do nothing, it's none of your business?
- do nothing because you weren't sure what to do?
- tell a teacher?
- try to help in some other way?

If you saw someone in your class being bullied or picked on, would you:
- do nothing, it's none of your business?
- do nothing because you weren't sure what to do?
- tell a teacher?
- suggest they went to the peer counselling service?
- try to help in some other way?.

Alternatively, value statements could be included, such as

Students should always try to help each other
- strongly agree
- agree
- disagree
- strongly disagree

It's none of my business if someone else is unhappy
- strongly agree
- agree
- disagree
- strongly disagree

You should sort out your own problems
- strongly agree
- agree

- disagree
- strongly disagree

Talking about problems with someone else can help
- strongly agree
- agree
- disagree
- strongly disagree

If I see someone being bullied and do nothing about it then my behaviour is as bad as the bully's
- strongly agree
- agree
- disagree
- strongly disagree

The type of information yielded by this type of question could be used to work out a social attitude scale for the school. Comparison of whole-school results on an annual basis could reflect change at an organisational level. Studies of school effectiveness (Brookover *et al.*, 1979; Rutter *et al.*, 1979; Mortimore *et al.*, 1988) have included measures of "social climate". In Brookover's study social climate was based upon a combination of pupil- teacher- and head-based variables. Pupil–climate variables included sense of academic futility, career expectations and appreciation of current education. Rutter *et al.* (1979) looked at, amongst many other factors, the extent to which students were given responsibility and the stability of the student's circle of friends. The correlation between student responsibility and good exam results was high. Mortimore *et al.* (1988) looked at "non-cognitive outcomes" of the educational system for students, using student reports on attitudes towards school and education, social relationships and self-image to do this.

An important consideration here is that the pre- post-test research design involves the notion of first identifying needs and objectives in a specific setting and then developing instruments to determine whether the programme has met those needs or achieved its objectives. A common difficulty is that very often there is no control group with which to make comparisons. Most problematic of all, it is certain to be difficult for the researcher to determine whether changes took place as a result of the peer counselling programme itself, whether they would have taken place anyway or whether improvements actually resulted from the experience of taking part in a project led by an enthusiastic team (the

"Hawthorne effect").

Another common research design uses the *self-report method* of evaluation. Here participants complete checklists or questionnaires to see if the programme achieved its aims and objectives. This method is likely to give leaders useful feedback and should be a natural extension of the evaluation and monitoring of any intervention such as peer counselling. However, it too relies on a clear identification of aims and objectives by the initiators of the programme; this in itself can be difficult to achieve since the flexible nature of many peer counselling programmes often means that the aims change as the needs of the clients become more evident.

The widely-used *case study method* captures the unique qualities of a programme and is usually rich in anecdotal detail. Practitioners find case studies helpful and insightful, and they have value for researchers in identifying the important issues which emerge during the life of a project. It may be difficult to make comparisons between projects and to make broad generalisations from a particular case, but case studies can highlight strengths and weaknesses in any programme if a range of perspectives is elicited and if participants are encouraged to be reflective and constructively critical. The case study method continues to be useful for evaluation studies in which we need to find answers to the questions "how" and "why" in contexts where the researcher has little control over the events as they occur. For a useful guide to this method see Yin (1994).

Where are we now?

Earlier research on peers helping peers focussed on the role of young people as academic tutors. Most studies showed a consistent tendency for peer tutoring programmes to give effective support to students who were experiencing difficulties in their studies. As we have shown in this book, we can now state with some confidence that peers also have a part to play in alleviating more personal and social problems, such as family difficulties, relationship difficulties and friendship problems within the peer group. The rationale of such programmes is usually that peers are more able to access young people in trouble, that peers have time to listen, that they have the language and shared culture to facilitate contact. There is certainly evidence that adolescents will disclose personal issues to a peer that they would not tell to a parent or teacher (Smith and Sharp, 1994). There appear to be clear benefits to schools where peer counselling takes place. De Rosenroll (1989) and Konet (1991), as we saw in Chapter 2, suggest that the advantages for schools include the creation of a helping role for students, the creation of opportunities for young people to learn about leadership and citizenship in a practical way, and a general enrichment of the whole school ethos as pupils and adults become more in tune with themselves and others in the school community. These views are confirmed by interviews with students and teachers alike as they spontaneously state the improvement in relationships and the greater sense of cooperation and mutual sharing which emerges in a community where values of prosocial behaviour and concern for others are actively promoted in a consistent way at all levels in the school.

There are benefits to the client groups. As we saw in Chapter 2, there is now a body of research which indicates measurable increases in such qualities as self-esteem amongst those students who have had a certain amount of contact time with a peer counsellor. There are also examples of reports from clients and potential clients of the satisfaction which they report in peer counselling services. The peer counsellors benefit in terms of qualities such as heightened self-esteem, social maturity and increased capacity to communicate effectively with their peers.

While most people in the field agree that there is still a need for systematic research studies to evaluate specific aspects of peer counselling, it is also clear that peer help programmes are difficult to evaluate because of the complex interplay of many different factors and processes. Furthermore, as we have seen in our own case studies in Part II of this book, the programmes themselves are usually in a state of change and development. Where the young people themselves are firmly established as innovators and organisers, it is highly likely that the structures will be changed as the programme develops and as new peer counsellors enter the system. This poses difficulties for the researcher when it comes to evaluating outcomes and making comparisons between programmes.

Where do we go next?

As we have already indicated, there are three essential aspects of peer counselling evaluation:

- assessment of the self as helper
- assessment of knowledge and skills used in the process
- assessment of outcome.

But these invite further questions. In particular, they lead to questions about the kinds of problems and concerns which young people will bring to a peer counsellor, the kinds of problems with which peer counsellors are most competent to deal, the satisfaction or otherwise of clients with the service which they receive, the characteristics of the adults who facilitate and foster such programmes, the role of the whole school in developing policies to sustain and encourage such programmes, the long-term benefits to the school as a community, gender issues in training, models of counselling and peer support, and a host of others.

Evaluation, if it is to meet the needs of both practitioners and researchers, should focus on a range of issues. It is important, despite the difficulties, to assess the *outcomes* of a peer-led programme, for example by measuring changes in attitudes or levels of maturity and social responsibility, capacity for perspective-taking and communication skills. It is also essential to devise research which can investigate the *processes* which take place, how they influence the outcomes and what effect they have on all participants. It is also necessary to understand the *systems* which facilitate such innovatory practices by, for example, examining the personal qualities of the charismatic individuals who often lead such interventions, their role in the school management structure, the nature of the policies in the schools and the links with the wider community. It is also interesting to evaluate the relationship between facilitator and participants, and to explore the interactions among participants at all levels of communication. This can be done with careful documentation of input and output effects at each stage of the programme.

In the previous chapter, we outlined some evaluation strategies which practitioners themselves can usefully incorporate into the design of an intervention. In this last chapter we have pointed out the strengths and weaknesses of a number of research strategies for evaluating the effectiveness of a peer counselling intervention.

Finally, we hope that readers of this book will work on to involve students in peer support activities and will learn through this experience the potential for achieving more constructive relationships, social responsibility and a sense of community. Research from the United States suggests that an increasing number of young people are at risk of destructive social and health behaviours (Dryfoos, 1990). The Consortium for the Promotion of School Based Competence (1994) quote statistics which suggest that in North America young people are less prepared to assume responsible places in society than their parents were. Given "the more complex and competitive nature" of their society they view this as extremely worrying, and acknowledge schools as the key context within which positive action to promote social competence can occur. They write:

> In contrast to other potential sites for intervention, schools provide access to all children on a regular and consistent basis over the majority of their formative years of personality development. (Consortium, 1994, p. 278)

> Schools as organisations enjoy unequaled influence – both formalised and unformalised – in children's lives with respect to social, moral, intellectual and behavioural development. With respect to social adjustment, schools are particularly well suited as sites to promote children's development. (p. 279)

We would suggest that peer support systems provide an example of how schools can achieve such influence in a realistic and practical way. We end with a quote from the Seville Statement on Violence:

> Just as "wars begin in the minds of men", peace also begins in our minds. The same species who invented war is capable of inventing peace. The responsibility lies with each of us. (UNESCO, 1986)

References

Anderson, T. (1987) "The reflecting team: dialogue and meta-dialogue in clinical work", *Family Process*, **26,** 415–28.

Araki, D., Takeshita, C. and Kadomoto, L. (1989) *Research Results and Final Report for the "Dispute Management in the Schools" Project* (Honolulu: Program on Conflict Resolution, University of Hawaii at Manoa).

Arora, T. (1989) "Bullying – action and intervention", *Pastoral Care in Education*, **7**, 44–7.

Barnes, T. and Austin, A. M. (1991) *The Influences of Parents and Siblings on the Development of a Personal Premise System in Middle Childhood*, paper presented at the biennial meeting of the Society for Research in Child Development (April), Seattle, WA.

Besag, V. (1989) *Bullies and Victims in Schools* (Milton Keynes: Open University Press).

Boehm, K., Chessare, J., Valko, T. and Sager, M. (1991) "Teen Line", *Adolescence*, **26** (103), 643–8.

Bowlby (1988) "Developmental psychiatry comes of age", *American Journal of Psychiatry*, **145**, 1–10.

Brier, J. and Ahmad, Y. (1991) "Developing a school court as a means of addressing bullying in schools" in P. K. Smith and D. A. Thompson (eds.) *Practical Approaches to Bullying* (London: David Fulton).

Brookover, W., Beady, C., Flood, P., Schweitzer, J. and Wisenbaker, J. (1979) *School Social Systems and Student Achievement: Schools Can Make a Difference* (New York: Praeger).

Carr, R. (1988) "The city-wide peer counselling program", *Children and Youth Services Review*, **10** (3), 217–32.

Carr, R. (1994) "Peer helping in Canada", *Peer Counselling Journal*, **11** (1), 6–9.

Carr, R. and Saunders, G. A. K. (1980) *Peer Counselling Starter Kit* (Victoria, BC: Peer Counselling Project, University of Victoria).

Carr, W. (1991) "Education for citizenship", *British Journal of Educational Studies*, **39** (4), 373–85.

Cicirelli, V. G. (1976) "Siblings teaching siblings" in V. L. Allen (ed.) *Children as Teachers: Theory and Research on Tutoring* (New York: Academic Press).

Consortium for the Promotion of School Based Competence, The (1994) "The school based promotion of social competence: theory, research, practice and policy" in R. J. Haggerty, L. R. Sherrod, N. Garmezy and M. Rutter (eds.) *Stress, Risk and Resilience in Children and Adolescents: Processes, Mechanisms and Interventions* (New York: Cambridge University Press).

Cowie, H., Smith, P. K., Boulton, M. and Laver, R. (1994) *Cooperation in the Multi-ethnic Classroom* (London: David Fulton).

DeCecco, J. and Richards, A. (1974) *Growing Pains: Uses of School Conflict* (New York: Aberdeen Press).

De Rosenroll, D. (1989) "A practitioner's guide to peer counselling research issues and dilemmas", *Canadian Journal of Counselling*, **23** (1), 75–91.

De Waal, F. (1992) "Aggression as a well-integrated part of primate social relationships: a critique of the Seville Statement on violence" in J. Silverberg and J. P. Gray (eds.) *Aggression and Peacefulness in Humans and Other Primates* (Oxford: Oxford University Press).

Dowling, E. and Osbourne, E. (eds.) (1985) *The Family and the School: A joint systems approach to problems with children* (London: Routledge and Kegan Paul).

Dryfoos, J. G. (1990) *Adolescents at Risk: Prevalence and Prevention* (New York: Oxford University Press).

Duck, S. W. (1991) *Friends for Life* (Hemel Hempstead: Harvester-Wheatsheaf).

Dunn, J. (1983) "Sibling relationships in early childhood", *Child Development*, **54**, 787–811.

Dunn, J. (1988) *The Beginnings of Social Understanding* (Oxford: Blackwell).

Dunn, J., Brown, J. R. and Beardsall, L. (1991) "Family talk about emotions, and children's later understanding of others' emotions", *Developmental Psychology* **27**, 448–55.

Egan, G. (1990) *The Skilled Helper* (Pacific Grove, CA: Brooks Cole).

Elton, R. E. (Lord) (1989) *Discipline in Schools: The report of the committee chaired by Lord Elton* (Norwich: HMSO/DES).

Eslea, M. and Smith, P. K. (1995) *Attitudes Toward Bullying in Primary School Pupils and Parents*, poster presented to the annual conference of the British Psychological Society (April), University of Warwick.

Frey, D. (1991) *100 Inspirational Quotations for Enhancing Self esteem* (Dayton, OH: self-published).

Goodall, J. (1986) *The Chimpanzees of Gombe: Patterns of behaviour* (Cambridge, MA: Harvard University Press).

Gougeon, C. (1989) "Guidelines for special issues training sessions in secondary school peer counselling programs", *Canadian Journal of Counselling*, **23** (1), 120–6.

Gray, R. E. (1988) "The role of school counselors with bereaved teenagers with and without support groups", *The School Counselor*, **35** (3), 185–93.

Guttman, M. A. J. (1985) "A peer counselling model: social outreach", *Canadian Counsellor*, **19** (3-4), 135–43.

Hartup, W. W. (1992) "Conflict and friendship relations" in C. U. Shantz and W. W. Hartup (eds.) *Conflict in Child and Adolescent Development* (New York: Cambridge University Press).

Hattie, J. A. (1975) "Youthline Dunedin: an evaluation of a telephone counselling service", *NZ Medical Journal*, **82**, 80–1.

Helmstetter, E., Peck, C. A. and Giangreco, M. F. (1994) "Outcomes of interactions with peers with moderate or severe difficulties: a stateside survey of high school students", *Journal of the Association for Persons with Severe*

Handicap, **19** (4), 263–76.

Henrikson, E. (1991) "A peer helping program for the middle school", *Canadian Journal of Counselling*, **25** (1), 12–18.

Inskipp, F. (1986) *Counselling: the Trainer's Handbook* (Cambridge: National Extension College).

James, J., Charlton, T., Leo, E. and Indoe, D. (1991) "A peer to listen", *Support for Learning*, **6** (4), 165–9.

Judge, P. G. (1991) "Dyadic and triadic reconciliations in pigtail macaques (Macau nemestrina)", *American Journal of Primatology*, **23**, 225–37.

Kagan, N. and Kagan, H. (1991) "Interpersonal process recall" in P. Dowrick (ed.) *Practical Guide to Using Video in the Behavioural Sciences* (New York: Wiley).

Katz, L. F., Kramer, L. and Gottman, J. M. (1992) "Conflict and emotion in marital, sibling and peer relationships" in C. V. Shantz and W. W. Hartup (eds.) *Conflict in Child and Adolescent Development* (New York: Cambridge University Press).

Kennedy, E., and Charles, S. C. (1977) *On Becoming a Counsellor: A basic guide for non-professional counsellors* (Dublin: Gill and Macmillan Ltd).

Konet, R. (1991) "Peer helpers in the middle school", *Middle School Journal*, September, 13–16.

Kramer, L. and Baron, L. A. (1995) "Intergenerational linkages: how experiences with siblings relate to the parenting of siblings", *Journal of Social and Personal Relationships*, **12** (1), 67–87.

Kreidler, W. J. (1984) *Creative Conflict Resolution* (Glenview, IL: Goodyear).

Lane, P., McWhirter, J. and Jeffries, J. (1992) "A peer mediation model: conflict resolution for elementary and middle school children", *Elementary School Guidance and Counseling*, **27** (1), 15–23.

Laursen, B. (1993) "The perceived impact of conflict on adolescent relationships", *Merrill-Palmer Quarterly*, **39** (4), 535–50.

Lawrence, D. (1981) "The development of a self-esteem questionnaire", *British Journal of Educational Psychology*, **51**, 245–51.

Main, M., Kaplan, N. and Cassidy, J. (1985) "Security in infancy, childhood and adulthood: a move to the level of representation" in J. Bretherton and E. Waters (eds.) *Growing Points of Attachment Theory and Research: Monographs of the Society for Research in Child Development*, **50** (1–2, Serial No. 209).

Marcoux, Y. and Kiely, M. (1985) "Early loss and adult personality", *Bereavement Care (Cruse)*, **4** (1), 3–4.

McCormick, M. (1988) *Mediation in the Schools: An evaluation of the Wakefield pilot peer mediation in Tucson, Arizona* (Washington, DC: American Bar Association).

McGrath, H., and Francey, S. (1991) *Friendly Kids, Friendly Classrooms* (Melbourne: Longman Cheshire).

McGuire, A. (1994) "Helping behaviors in the natural environment: dimensions and correlates of helping", *Personality and Social Psychology Bulletin*, **20** (1), 45–56.

Minuchin, S. (1974) *Families and Family Therapy* (Cambridge, MA: Harvard University Press).

Mortimore, P., Sammons, P., Stoll, L., Lewis, D. and Ecob, R. (1988) *School Matters: The junior years* (Wells, Somerset: Open Books Publishing Ltd).

Murfitt, J. and Thomas, J. (1983) "The effects of peer-counselling on the self-concept and reading attainments of secondary aged slow learning pupils", *Remedial Education*, **18**, 73–4.

Neville, M. (1995) "Circles network" in A. Wertheimer (ed.) *Circles of Support: Building inclusive communities* (Bristol: Circles Network).

Newton, C., Taylor, G. and Wilson, D. (1996) "Circle of Friends: an inclusive approach to meeting emotional and behavioural needs", *Educational Psychology in Practice* (in press).

Nowicki, S. and Strickland, B. (1973) "A locus of control scale for children", *Journal of Consulting and Clinical Psychology*, **40**, 148–54.

Olweus, D. (1994) "Bullying at school: basic facts and effects of a school-based intervention program", *Journal of Child Psychology and Psychiatry*, **35** (7), 1171–90.

Pearpoint, J., Forest, M. and Snow, J. (1992) *The Inclusion Papers* (London: Inclusion Press).

Pearson, J. (1995) *Telecounselling Access, Anonymity and Advocacy*, paper presented at the International Conference on Child Peer Relationships (January), University of South Australia, Adelaide.

Perske, R. (1988) *Circle of Friends* (London: Abingdon Press).

Pitfield, M. (1992) *An Investigation into, Interest in, and Effectiveness of Bully Courts*, unpublished BA dissertation, University of Sheffield.

Putallaz, M., Costanzo, P. R. and Smith, R. B. (1991) "Maternal recollections of childhood peer relationships: implications for their children's social competence", *Journal of Social and Personal Relationships*, **8**, 403–22.

Quarmby, D. (1993) "Peer counselling with bereaved adolescents", *British Journal of Guidance and Counselling*, **21** (2), 196–211.

Ross, H. G. and Milgram, J. I. (1982) "Important variables in adult sibling relationships" in M. E. Lamb and B. Sutton-Smith (eds.) *Sibling Relationships: Their Nature and Significance Across the Lifespan* (Hillsdale, NJ: Lawrence Erlbaum Associates).

Rutter, M., Maughan, B., Mortimore, P., Oustan, J. and Smith, A. (1979) *Fifteen Thousand Hours: Secondary schools and their effects on children.* (Cambridge, MA: Harvard Unversity Press).

Scaife, J. M. (1993) "Application of a general supervision framework: creating a context of co-operation", *Educational and Child Psychology*, **10** (2), 61–72.

Selman, R. L. (1980) *The Growth of Interpersonal Understanding* (New York: Academic Press).

Shantz, C. U. (1983) "Social cognition" in J. H. Flavell and E. M. Markman (eds.) *Handbook of Child Psychology: Cognitive Development*, vol. 3, 4th edition (New York: Wiley).

Sharp, S., Sellors, A. and Cowie, H. (1994) "Time to listen: setting up a peer counselling service to help tackle the problem of bullying in schools", *Pastoral Care in Education*, **12** (2), 3–6.

Smith, P. K. and Sharp, S. (1994) *School Bullying: Insights and perspectives* (London: Routledge).

Smucny, D. and Aureli, F. (1994) *Reconciliation Roundtable Summary* (personal communication).

Snyder, A. (1988) *A Young People's Guide to Co-Counselling* (Seattle: Re-evaluation Counselling).

Sprinthall, N., Hall, J. and Gerber, E. (1992) "Peer counselling for middle school students experiencing family divorce: a deliberate psychological education model", *Elementary School Guidance and Counselling*, **26** (4) 279–94.

Stewart, R. B. (1983) "Sibling attachment relationships: child–infant interactions in the Strange Situation", *Developmental Psychology*, **19**, 192–9.

Tattum, D. and Herbert, G. (1990) *Bullying: A positive response* (Cardiff: South Glamorgan Institute of Education).

Thompson, D. A. and Sharp, S. (1994) *Improving Schools: Integrating whole school behaviour policies* (London: David Fulton).

Tindall, J. and Gray, H. (1985) *Becoming an Effective Peer Helper: Book 1 Introductory Program*, 2nd edition (Muncie, IN: Accelerated Development Press).

Trevarthen, C. and Logotheti, K. (1989) "Child in society, and society in children: the nature of basic trust" in S. Howell and R. Willis (eds.) *Societies at Peace* (London: Routledge).

UNESCO (1986) "The Seville statement on violence" in J. Silverberg and J. P. Gray (eds.) (1992) *Aggression and Peacefulness in Humans and Other Primates* (Oxford: Oxford University Press).

Weissner, T. S. and Gallimore, R. (1977) "My brother's keeper: child and sibling caretaking", *Current Anthropology*, **18**, 169–90.

Whitney, I. and Smith, P. K. (1993) "A survey of the nature and extent of bullying in junior/middle and secondary schools", *Educational Research*, **35** (1), 3–25.

Winnicott, D. W. (1984) *The Child, the Family and the Outside World* (London: Penguin Books).

Yin, R. (1994) *Case Study Research* (London: Sage).

INDEX